Mañjuśrī's Heart Advice

Mañjuśrī's Heart Advice

Khenchen Appey Rinpoche's Oral Instructions on *Parting from the Four Attachments*

Including Translations of
Sakya Paṇḍita's *Oral Instructions on Parting From the Four Attachments*
Gorampa Sönam Sengé's Commentary
A Key to the Profound Essential Points
& Jamyang Khyentse Wangpo's Song of Experience
Nectar from the Heart

VAJRA
Publications Inc.Pvt.Ltd.

Published and Distributed 2025 by
Vajra Publications Inc.Pvt.Ltd.
Jyatha, Thamel, P.O. Box 21779, Kathmandu, Nepal
Tel.: 977-1-5320562
e-mail: vajrabooksktm@gmail.com
www.vajrabookshop.com

© 2025 by Christian Bernert, Chödung Karmo Translation Group
This book is in copyright. No part of this book may be reproduced or utilized in any form or by any means, electronic or mechanical, including photocopying, recording or by any information storage or retrieval system, without permission in writing from the author or the publisher.

ISBN: 978-9937-624-55-8

Printed in Nepal

NGOR LUDING LADRANG

P.O. Manduwala,
Dehradun - 248007
Uttarakhand, India

Foreword

Over two thousand five hundred years ago, Buddha Śākyamuni stated:

> Commit not even a single misdeed,
> Accumulate a wealth of virtue,
> And perfectly tame your mind—
> That is the teaching of the Buddha.

These words are true not only for the individual person but also on the level of society in general, for individual communities and for entire nations, regardless of religious or secular orientation. In brief, whether considering oneself, others, or all beings—here and now, or in our short-term or distant future—the Buddha clearly taught that freedom and peace depend on whether we have tamed our mind.

Not only is the practice of mind training the essence of the bodhisattva path, the principal method to tame one's mind, and the heart of the Buddhist path in general, it is also the practice that has the greatest impact on our happiness and peace. Moreover, the practice of mind training is extremely helpful in bringing about peace in society and in strengthening our confidence in the face of the many difficulties of life—all our struggles, anxieties, worries, and fears.

In terms of the two most renowned traditions of mind training, the present publication contains Khenchen Appey Rinpoche Ngawang Yönten Zangpo's teachings on *Parting from the Four Attachments*, which the Protector Mañjughoṣa bestowed on Sachen Kunga Nyingpo. These teachings were originally given at the International Buddhist Academy in Kathmandu, and it is worthy of praise that they have now been translated into English.

We conclude with the following words of aspiration from Ngorchen Kunga Zangpo:

> Having ascertained the truth that, from the very beginning,
> all phenomena are like dreams and magical illusions—appearing, yet empty of true existence—
> Grant your blessing that the genuine path of union's middle way,
> Free of all grasping, may arise within the mind.

Sharchen Ludingpa Chökyi Gyaltsen wrote this at Ngor Evaṃ, the main seat of the Ngor tradition in India, on the 15th day of the first month of the year of the Wood Snake of the 17th *rabjung* cycle (March 14, 2025).

Contents

Foreword by Luding Khen Rinpoche	v
Introduction	xi
Oral Instructions on Parting from the Four Attachments by Sakya Paṇḍita Kunga Gyaltsen	1
A Key to the Profound Essential Points by Gorampa Sönam Sengé	3
Nectar from the Heart by Jamyang Khyentse Wangpo	19

Khenchen Appey Rinpoche's Commentary

Outline of the Teaching	25
Introductory Teachings	29
The Main Part of the Teaching on *Parting from the Four Attachments*	59
"If You are Attached to This Life, You are Not a Dharma Practitioner."	65

"If You Are Attached to Saṃsāra,
    You Have No Renunciation."   95

"If You Are Attached to Your Own Self-Interest,
    You Have No Bodhicitta."   117

"If There Is Grasping, It Is Not The View."   155

Concluding Words of Advice   187

Endnotes   195

Glossary   203

Bibliography   237

Ārya Mañjuśrī (Courtesy of Enlightenment Thangka)

Introduction

The profound teaching known as *Parting from the Four Attachments* represents a quintessential moment of Buddhist wisdom. In just four lines of instructions, the bodhisattva Mañjuśrī transmitted to the young Sachen Kunga Nyingpo the very essence of Buddhist practice. As Khenchen Appey Rinpoche explains: "When the Great Lama Sakyapa Kunga Nyingpo was twelve years old, he stayed in retreat for six months to practice the sādhana of Mañjughoṣa. At one point during this retreat, he had a direct vision of the protector Mañjughoṣa, who uttered the following lines:

> If you are attached to this life, you are not a Dharma practitioner.
> If you are attached to saṃsāra, you have no renunciation.
> If you are attached to your own self-interest, you have no bodhicitta.
> If there is grasping, it is not the view.

With these four lines, Mañjughoṣa Pāramitāyāna practice in its entirety."

Historical Context

To fully appreciate the importance of this teaching, it is helpful to understand its place in history. The first golden age of Buddhism in Tibet occurred between the seventh and ninth centuries, when Tibet was considered a unified kingdom under the rulership of the three Dharma kings Songtsen Gampo, Trisong Detsen, and Tri Ralpachen.[1] After the collapse of the Tibetan empire in the ninth century, different regions and rising aristocratic families became patrons of various Buddhist traditions. This period witnessed what is referred to as the "Second Diffusion" of Buddhism in Tibet, characterized by a rich exchange between Indian masters and their Tibetan Dharma heirs, prolific translation activity, and the emergence of new Buddhist traditions.[2]

One family that played an important role in this renaissance was the Khön family, a clan long associated with the early lineage of Buddhism introduced in the seventh century. Khön Lui Wangpo was, in fact, one of the twenty-five principal disciples of Padmasambhava and one of the first seven Tibetans to ordain as Buddhist monks under Śāntarakṣita in the eighth century. By the eleventh century, the general state of religious practice and transmission in Tibet had declined to a point where a descendant of Lui Wangpo, Khön Könchok Gyalpo, decided to seek out tantric teachings from new sources. One event in particular, the public performance of a tantric ritual in a marketplace, is said to have precipitated this decision. In 1073, he proceeded to establish a temple in the small town of Sakya, as the seat for the new tradition. It was at this seat where Khön Könchok Gyalpo's son, Kunga Nyingpo, built on his father's legacy, receiving further tantric lineages and transmitting them to his heirs. He is therefore recognized as the first founding master of the new tradition from Sakya and referred to as "Sachen," the great (*chen*) master of Sakya (*sa*).

Sachen Kunga Nyingpo

Sachen's early education began under his father, Könchok Gyalpo, from whom he received the three Hevajra tantras.³ After his father's death, when Sachen was eleven, the renowned translator Bari Lotsāwa temporarily took the Sakya throne and oversaw Sachen's further education. It was under his guidance that Sachen underwent the above-mentioned six-month retreat, during which he received the instructions on *Parting from the Four Attachments* directly from Mañjuśrī. Throughout his youth, Sachen studied under numerous prominent teachers. These include Darma Nyingpo, from whom he received teachings on Abhidharma; Zhangtön Chöbar, who would later transmit the Lamdré teachings to him; his paternal relative Khön Gyichu Dralhawar, under whom we received another Hevajra lineage and teachings on Cakrasaṃvara; and Mal Lotsāwa Lodrö Drakpa, who was an important holder of the Vajrayoginī lineage and many other teachings. In the middle of these formative years, the then elderly Bari Lotsāwa appointed Sachen as the throne holder of Sakya, when he had reached the age of twenty.

A pivotal moment in Sachen's life came when he sought the complete transmission of the Lamdré teachings from Zhangtön Chöbar. Initially reluctant, Zhangtön eventually agreed to transmit the teachings to Sachen. The transmission was extensive, taking eight years to complete, with Zhangtön advising Sachen not to even mention the name "Lamdré" for eighteen years, let alone teach it to others. After this period, he was free to teach or write commentaries on its profound instructions if he so wished. Following this advice, Sachen spent the next eighteen years meditating on the teachings. At age forty-six, he had a vision in which the Mahāsiddha Virūpa himself bestowed the transmission upon him. Sachen then began teaching Lamdré and writing about it from the age of forty-nine. He is credited with being the first to write down Virūpa's *Vajra Verses*, the foundational text for the Lamdré tradition, which until this point was passed down as an oral lineage. He also wrote eleven commentaries on this text.

A dramatic episode in Sachen's life occurred when a sickness left him in a coma and caused complete memory loss. Although he recovered most of his teachings by receiving them again from various masters, he had no one to request the Lamdré teachings from. He therefore went into retreat and prayed to his guru, and was able to remember some of the lost teachings. Later, Zhangtön Chöbar appeared to him in a dream and transmitted the remainder. After recovering his knowledge, he had further visions of Virūpa who transmitted further teachings and empowerments.

Sachen Kunga Nyingpo had four sons: Lopön Sönam Tsemo and Jetsün Drakpa Gyaltsen, who succeeded him as Sakya throne holders; Kungabar, who died young while returning from studies in India; and Palchen Wöpo, would become the father of the renowned Sakya Paṇḍita Kunga Gyaltsen, the fourth throne holder of Sakya.

Sachen died in 1158 at the age of sixty-seven, leaving behind a prolific legacy of scholarship and practice.

Mind Training Traditions in Tibet

Parting from the Four Attachments belongs to the class of mind training instructions, or *lojong* in Tibetan. These are generally brief, practice-oriented teachings that strike at the very heart of the matter without going into elaborate, philosophical explanations. Many Mahāyāna pith instructions were transmitted in Tibet.[4] "Among these," as Appey Rinpoche explains, "the two most famous ones are the lojong mind training teachings given by Serlingpa to Jowo Jé Palden Atiśa and the pith instructions on *Parting from the Four Attachments*, which the noble Mañjughoṣa imparted to Sachen Kunga Nyingpo."

Atiśa's influence on the development of Buddhism in Tibet can hardly be overstated. Originally from Bengal, he travelled to a far island of Southeast Asia, probably Sumatra, to study mind training for twelve years under Serlingpa, the master from the "Golden Island." Later in life, he was invited to Tibet by Lha Lama Yeshe Ö, a ruler of the Gugé Kingdom in Southwest Tibet, and his nephew Jangchub Ö. This happened in the eleventh century, the time after the fall of the Tibetan empire that marked the beginning of the second transmission of Buddhism. As mentioned above, the havoc caused by the last emperor Langdarma brought with it a general decline in the Dharma and with it, apparently, a great deal of confusion as to how to integrate the various teachings and systems of practice into one coherent path. To remedy this situation, the king sought Atiśa's guidance. His teachings emphasize the importance of gradual training in the stages of the path and mind training rooted in bodhicitta. Some of the most revered and still widely taught texts to emerge from his tradition are Atiśa's own *Lamp for the Path to Awakening*, which became the source text for the entire Lamrim genre ("stages of the path") particularly popular in the Geluk tradition, and the lojong text *Mind Training in Seven Points* compiled by Chekawa Yeshe Dorje, which is said to contain the essence of Serlingpa's instructions.[5]

The second lojong tradition mentioned by Khenchen Appey Rinpoche comes from the four statements Sachen Kunga Nyingpo received from Mañjuśrī. The outstanding feature of these instructions is their ability to convey profound points with exceptional brevity—a quality that has certainly contributed to their widespread popularity. By just remembering four lines, the theory and practice of the entire path of the Pāramitāyāna can be unpacked. In this sense, they are like four magic keys that unlock increasingly deeper levels of authentic Dharma practice.

The Structure of the Teaching

To understand how these brief instructions encompass the entire path, we must examine how each line builds upon the previous one, creating a complete framework for practice. This structure is clearly revealed in Jamyang Khyentse Wangpo's *Song of Experience*, also included in the present volume.

Each of the four statements represents a profound challenge to ordinary modes of perception and is designed to reveal and dismantle the fundamental mechanisms of suffering. Reading them may initially stir up a sense of unease, indicating how deeply ingrained the patterns obstructing awakening really are.

> *"If you are attached to this life, you are not a Dharma practitioner."*

This first line may be the hardest pill to swallow. It questions not only the relationship we have to our own life and body, but also the nature of our practice: "How could I not be attached to my life? After all, this is all I have. How does attachment to my life make me not a genuine practitioner? Am I on the right track with my practice?" These are important questions to ask, if we are to take the path seriously.

Here, it is helpful to recall the first of the four seals of the Buddhist view: "All compounded phenomena are impermanent." Appreciating the impermanence of life can be a deeply transformative experience that fundamentally restructures our priorities. It has profound implications for the way we relate to ourselves and others, as Drakpa Gyaltsen poignantly points out in his commentary.[6]

One important notion underpinning this teaching is the belief in rebirth. Within the Buddhist context, it is presupposed that an individual's experience encompasses not only the present life but also past and future existences. Although this is not the place to explore this subject in detail, the following question may be raised: Assuming we accept that nothing in the world comes from nothingness and that nothing vanishes into nonexistence, why would consciousness, or awareness, cease to exist when the body dies and gradually disintegrates back into its constituent elements? Even though there is no solid proof to either establish or deny rebirth indisputably, there seem to be many indications supporting its existence. These include unexplainable yet verifiable past life memories of children with no prior exposure to the concept of rebirth, strong psychological predispositions in certain individuals that cannot be explained based on experiences in this life alone, memories of experienced meditators, recollections induced by hypnosis, accounts of near-death experiences, and so forth. In Buddhism, one is not required to blindly believe anything. The idea of rebirth is therefore to be accepted on trust (that is, trust based on the trustworthiness of the verifiable teachings of the Buddha, such as his explanations on ethical conduct, meditation, and insight) and as a working hypothesis.

In terms of traditional contemplations, the first line relates to the reflections on the precious nature of a human life endowed with the opportunity to practice Dharma, of its impermanence, and of the fact that no material wealth or worldly recognition will be of help at the time of death. By giving up an unrealistic and unskillful relationship to our life, we establish the foundations for genuine Dharma practice.

"If you are attached to saṃsāra, you have no renunciation."

Having accepted that ambitions and gains limited to this life are not worth the trouble, we are led to question further: "What, then, is of true value?" This reflection invites a deeper look at the conditions compounding our experiences. "Saṃsāra" is not an external place we might be attached to; it is another name for experience conditioned by layers of desire, hatred, and ignorance, no matter how subtle. In this sense, it is explained that every experience conditioned in such ways is bound to fail to bring lasting satisfaction. This too may be difficult to digest.

The second seal authenticating the Buddhist view states: "All afflicted states are in the nature of suffering." The Buddhist understanding of suffering goes beyond the unpleasant; it includes the ultimately unsatisfactory nature of conditioned existence. This takes into account not only the objects of experience but, most importantly, the subjective conditioning of experience itself. As long as experience is conditioned by a fundamental misunderstanding of reality, nothing is ever really OK.

These reflections are based on two fundamental contemplations: the law of karma, that is, the universal principle that actions produce corresponding results, and the unsatisfactory nature of conditioned existence. Even though these thoughts are sometimes labelled "preliminary contemplations," they are foundational and therefore crucial for practice. Adopting a sober, bird's eye view on life and experience itself in this way may not be the most romantic thing to do, but it is said to mark the beginning of the actual path to liberation.

"If you are attached to your own self-interest, you have no bodhicitta."

After establishing the right priorities and clarifying the goal, the third line represents a profound shift of gears. It challenges the default mode of thinking that underlies even the wish to seek peace for oneself. The premise here is that, as long as the "I" is at the center of our efforts, our path is misguided and any benefits gained in this way are flawed in one way or another.

The teachings on bodhicitta related to this line lie at the very heart of the Mahāyāna tradition and the lojong teachings in particular. To overturn the driving force behind saṃsāra—the attitude of self-cherishing—we are instructed to soften and open the mind and heart by cultivating altruistic love, compassion, and bodhicitta. The most radical training that goes directly against the grain of our habitual mode of functioning is the exchange of oneself for others, sometimes called the secret practice of the bodhisattvas. This practice finds application not only in the safe environment of the meditation session, but also in daily life, the true testing ground for progress. Its ultimate benefit could not be more profound: complete awakening. However, this training represents only one side of the coin, and is traditionally referred to as the accumulation of merit. For these actions to become actual causes for enlightenment, they need to be imbued with the wisdom of the right view, which is the subject of the last line:

"If there is grasping, it is not the view."

This instruction challenges the most universal and subtle of all attachments: conceptual grasping. Since relating to the cognitive process at this level requires considerable lucidity and stability of mind, a first step must be training in calm abiding. It is taught that only a well-trained mind has the capacity to gain direct perception of the true nature of things, sustain that view, and integrate the experience in a beneficial way. This is what distinguishes genuine, liberative insight from intellectual understanding.

It is important to be aware that teaching the highest view entails several pitfalls. Khenchen Appey Rinpoche points out that if not taught skillfully, the view of emptiness may be completely misunderstood, causing the listener to lose trust in the Dharma in general, or to generate wrong views, such as the denial of conventional reality and the unfailing relationship between actions and their results. Such misunderstandings represent serious obstacles on the path.

The training in insight itself can be carried out in various ways, using analytical examination as taught in the Madhyamaka treatises, or analogies, as in the tradition of these pith instructions. Either way, the key point is to arrive at a view free of grasping, transcending all dualistic notions and conceptual extremes. This represents the culmination of the training that gradually unties the knots that bind us in saṃsāra, leading to the deepest level of freedom: freedom from all attachments and obscurations. Combined with the previous trainings, this view generates the powerful causes for complete awakening, the most profound way to benefit both oneself and others.

The Literature on Parting from the Four Attachments

The essential instructions Sachen received from Mañjuśrī were later elucidated by various teachers. The earliest written texts are Drakpa Gyaltsen's explanation, very experiential in nature, and Sakya Paṇḍita's concise instructions. Coming directly from

Sachen's son and grandson, these works are considered the most authoritative.

Later compositions based on the four lines include a commentary by Nupa Rigdzin Drak, a largely unknown author who may have been a disciple of Drakpa Gyaltsen; a lineage prayer by Ngorchen Kunga Zangpo, the founder of Ngor Evaṃ Chöden monastery; Ngorchen's detailed instructions written down by his disciple Kunga Lekrin; a practice manual by Ngorchen's disciple Gorampa Sönam Sengé; a song of realization by Jamyang Khyentse Wangpo, the great polymath and non-sectarian master of the nineteenth century; and a teaching manual by Ngor Pönlob Ngawang Lekdrup. These texts are preserved across three text collections compiled between the 15th and 19th centuries: Ngor Pönlob Loter Wangpo's Collection of Tantras, Jamgön Kongtrul's Treasury of Precious Instructions, and Müchen Könchok Gyaltsen's Hundred Instructions on Mind Training. They are also found in the collected works of the individual master.[7]

In addition to the above-mentioned writings, we find a short instruction manual by the Jonangpa Kunga Drolchok, which was mentioned by Khenchen Appey Rinpoche: "The Jonang master Kunga Drolchok collected the pith instructions of many Tibetan lineages and compiled them into what is known as the *Hundred Instructions from Jonang*. These include teachings from all four major schools of Tibetan Buddhism prevalent today. Kunga Drolchok felt that the teachings on *Parting from the Four Attachments* were the most beneficial for him to turn his mind to the Dharma. To acknowledge this, he placed these teachings at the very beginning of the collection."

Contemporary commentaries include an elaborate written commentary composed by Khenpo Tsultrim Palden from Litang, Eastern Tibet, now living in India, and the transcriptions of teachings by Chogye Trichen Rinpoche, the late head of the Tsarpa tradition, Dzongsar Khyentse Rinpoche, and, now, Khenchen Appey Rinpoche. The three modern spoken commentaries complement each other perfectly, with Khyentse Rinpoche's teaching given directly in English and representing the most current interpretation. Chogye Rinpoche's explanations are very much in the yogic tradition of Drakpa Gyaltsen, direct and experiential in nature, and Appey Rinpoche's approach, blends seamlessly pith instructions with lucid explanations of the theories behind the practice.

TRANSLATIONS IN THIS VOLUME

To set the stage for Khenchen Appey Rinpoche's oral commentary, we have included translations of three other texts from this cycle, each representing a distinct genre. The first is Sakya Paṇḍita's concise work, *Oral Instructions on Parting from the Four Attachments*. As one of the greatest luminaries in Tibetan Buddhist history and the grandson of Sachen Kunga Nyingpo, Sakya Paṇḍita brings considerable authority to this text. He expands on the implications of Mañjuśrī's four lines, illuminating both the pitfalls of the four attachments and the benefits of transcending them.

The second text is a practice manual by Gorampa Sönam Sengé, one of the most influential Sakya masters, whose rigorous philosophical writings are revered as one of the cornerstones of the Sakyapa view. His text, entitled *A Key to the Profound Essential Points*, begins by surveying the different approaches to general Mahāyāna practice found in the śāstras, or commentarial treatises, and the pith instruction traditions. He then turns to the mind training based on Mañjuśrī's four lines, offering detailed, practical guidance through each stage of cultivation. In his teaching, Khenchen Appey Rinpoche frequently referenced this text and strongly encouraged participants to study it.

The third text is *Nectar from the Heart*, a song of realization by Jamyang Khyentse Wangpo, the eminent 19th-century master who was instrumental in preserving and transmitting countless lineages across all traditions of Tibetan Buddhism. His elegant poem dedicates one stanza to each of Mañjuśrī's four lines, revealing both the significance of each step on the path and the limitations of each preceding accomplishment, ultimately guiding practitioners toward the highest achievement through realization of the ultimate view.

Khenchen Appey Rinpoche imparted the instructions that form that main part of this volume in June 2007, over the course of ten days, at the International Buddhist Academy (IBA) in Kathmandu, to an audience of Tibetan lamas, monastics, and international students. The teachings were orally translated into English by Khenpo Jamyang Tenzin, abbot of Mundgod Sakya monastery. Rinpoche's words were later transcribed in the original Tibetan and edited, partially by Rinpoche himself and the remainder by Khenpo Jamyang Tenzin, and were reviewed by khenpos Sönam Gyatso and Ngawang Jorden, principal of IBA. The second edition of the transcript, published in 2015, forms the basis for the present translation.

KHENCHEN APPEY RINPOCHE[8]

Early Life, Studies, and Teaching in Tibet

Born in 1927, Khenchen Appey Rinpoche was identified as the rebirth of the Kagyu master Khenchen Tsewang Paljor, who was considered to be an emanation of Marpa Lotsāwa, the great Tibetan translator and father of the Kagyu tradition. In his early childhood, the master Drupchen Adzom Rigdzin Mingyur Dorje bestowed the name "Appey" upon him, which he would keep for life. In his early years, two significant prophecies were made about him: first by Jamyang Khyentse Chökyi Lodrö, who predicted he would become a monk and benefit the teachings, and later by Khenchen Khedrup Sengé, who foresaw him becoming a great light for the Buddhist teachings.

His formal education began in 1935 when he entered Serjong Monastery. One important teacher in his early life was Jamgyal Rinpoche, abbot of Dzongsar Khamjé Shedra, from whom he received extensive instructions on Śāntideva's *The Way of the Bodhisattva*. He then soon joined Serjong Shedra, the monastery's college, where he studied for nine years under four great teachers. During this period, he gained renown for his scholarship and participated in public debates on sūtra, tantra, and traditional sciences. Around the year 1940, he received his novice vows from Khenchen Jamyang Gelek Palzang and the name Yönten Zangpo. By 1946, his scholarly achievements led to his appointment as a review teacher at Serjong Shedra.

Two years later, he joined Dzongsar Shedra where he studied philosophical treatises under Khenchen Thubten Gyaltsen for about three and a half years, further enhancing his reputation. He soon became a review teacher there as well.

A significant period in Rinpoche's life began in 1951 when he received numerous profound teachings from his root guru Khyentse Chökyi Lodrö, including the transmission of Lamdré Lobshé. His guru was so pleased with him that he bestowed upon him the name "spiritual friend who pleases Mañjuśrī, intelligence of the smiling son of Brahma."[9] That same year, he received full ordination vows from his guru Dezhung Anjam Rinpoche and the name Ngawang Yönten Zangpo. The following year, Rinpoche travelled to Dezhung where he received many teachings from Anjam Rinpoche, including

Overview of Tantra, *The Great Tree of Realization*, and the *Two Sections*.[10] Following the command of his guru Khyentse Chökyi Lodrö, Rinpoche spend the next year in retreat. From 1954 to 1957, he served as the abbot of Serjong Shedra.

Exile in India

Rinpoche's teaching career was interrupted by the political changes in Tibet in 1959, which led him to travel to Gangtok, Sikkim, where Jamyang Khyentse Chökyi Lodrö was residing at the time. There, his root guru made another prophecy, stating that he would become an eminent master and important upholder of the Sakya tradition. After his guru's passing in that same year, Rinpoche spent some time practicing meditation in sacred places.

In 1960, at the request of the Queen of Sikkim, he spent a year cataloging the scriptures of the Sakya tradition at the National Library of Sikkim. The following year was a period of intensive retreat practice for Rinpoche.

In 1963, Gongma Trichen Rinpoche, the 41st throne holder of the Sakya tradition, had relocated to the Dehradun area in Northern India and invited Appey Rinpoche to join him as his principal tutor. Over the course of the next few years, Rinpoche transmitted to him a great number of important teachings. In 1969, Rinpoche accepted the community's request to become principal of Ngor Evaṃ Shedrup Dargye Ling in Bir. During this time, he also established a center for studies and a center for practice, further developing the institution.

A crucial turning point came in 1972 when, following the vision of His Holiness Gongma Trichen, he established Sakya College. From 1973 to 1979, he taught numerous important treatises there, with his students including Dzongsar Khyentse Rinpoche, the rebirth of his root guru. Throughout this time, his dedication to the college's development continued, with Appey Rinpoche personally raising funds for new land and laying the foundations for a new campus. The 1980s saw him continuing his teaching activities at Sakya College, now relocated to Rajpur, while also maintaining his practice during intermittent periods of retreat. From 1985 to 1989, he divided his time between teaching Dharma, visiting various places to benefit beings, and staying in retreat in Pharping, Nepal.

Life in Nepal

The final two decades of Appey Rinpoche's life (1990–2010) were spent primarily in Nepal, maintaining a balance between teaching activities, including travels to Southeast Asia, and practice in retreat. During this period, he became increasingly aware of the need for a school that would make the Dharma accessible to non-Tibetan speakers, a project that would be supported by a devotee from Singapore.

In 2001, Rinpoche established the International Buddhist Academy (IBA) in Kathmandu, a school focused on making the Dharma accessible to international students through various programs, including teachings, translation initiatives, and publications, as well as education programs for Tibetan monastics. He also maintained connections with Tibet, funding extensive renovation projects at his home monastery, and preserved rare manuscripts through digitization and distribution.

Khenchen Appey Rinpoche retired to a private residence in Boudhanath, near to both IBA and the Great Stupa, where he always made himself available to those who sought his guidance, focusing especially on transmitting the teachings to lineage holders. He passed away on December 28, 2010, at approximately 9:30 in the morning, displaying his final teaching on impermanence.

Khenchen Appey Rinpoche left an enduring legacy. Renowned for his vast knowledge and the clarity of his teachings, he played an instrumental role in transmitting the precious teachings to a new generation of lineage holders and teachers, ensuring their continuation. He also played a crucial role in establishing and developing centers of learning for both Tibetan speakers and international students, and preserved a great collection of important texts for future generations. Despite his accomplishments, Rinpoche always exemplified humility, shunning public attention. He did not want people to prostrate to him and never referred to anyone as his student. Instead, he preferred to call those who studied under him his "Dharma friends." Embodying the ideal of a Buddhist master, wise and accomplished, his life itself served as an inspiration—a living testament to the Dharma.

ACKNOWLEDGEMENTS

This publication benefited from the contributions of many. We are particularly grateful to Khenpo Ngawang Jorden of IBA for his kind assistance in clarifying passages of Appey Rinpoche's teaching transcript. We also gratefully acknowledge Fundación Kunphen for sponsoring the editorial work, expertly handled by Sarah Teetor, and an anonymous donor in Hanoi for their generous contribution. Our thanks also go to Bess Hope and James Gattuso for their much-appreciated editorial work on the translation of Gorampa's commentary and the introduction, respectively, to the Khenpo Appey Foundation for their ongoing support, and to Vajra Publications in Kathmandu for their continued assistance with our publishing projects. Finally, we gratefully acknowledge Raju Yonjon from Enlightenment Thangka for providing us with the beautiful images included in this volume.

Dedication

We dedicate any merit generated through this publication
to the swift and complete accomplishment of the aspirations of Khenchen Appey Rinpoche,
to the long life and unobstructed activities of all those who uphold the true Dharma.
and to the temporary and ultimate happiness of all beings.

Christian Bernert
Chödung Karmo Translation Group
Hoi An, February 2025

Sachen Kunga Nyingpo (Courtesy of Enlightenment Thangka)

Oral Instructions on Parting from the Four Attachments

by Sakya Paṇḍita Kunga Gyaltsen

I prostrate at the feet of the sublime guru.

In general, having obtained a body endowed with freedoms and riches, having encountered the precious teachings of the Buddha, and having developed a genuine attitude, it is important to practice the true Dharma without error. For this, we must bring the instructions on parting from the four attachments into our experience.

What are these? Not being attached to this life; not being attached to the three realms of saṃsāra; not being attached to one's own benefit, and not being attached to things and characteristics.

To explain: This life is like a water bubble and the time of death is uncertain. It is therefore not worth being attached to it.

The three realms of saṃsāra are like poisonous fruit. Though delicious at first, they ultimately bring harm. Whoever is attached to them is deluded!

Being attached to one's own benefit is like nurturing the enemy's child. Though it may bring joy at first, it will certainly bring harm in the end. That being so, even if attachment to one's own benefit brings pleasure at first, it ultimately leads to the lower realms.

Clinging to things and characteristics is like mistaking a mirage for water. Though water appears at first, there is nothing to drink. Though saṃsāra appears to the confused mind, when examined with wisdom, nothing whatsoever is found to exist inherently. That being so, understanding how to disengage the mind from past and future, and how to disengage consciousness from the present, know all phenomena to be beyond elaboration.

In this way: Not being attached to this life, one will not be born in the lower realms. Not being attached to the three realms of saṃsāra, one will not be born in saṃsāra. Not being attached to one's own benefit, one will not be born as a śrāvaka or pratyekabuddha. Not being attached to things and characteristics, one will swiftly attain manifest and complete enlightenment.

This concludes the unerring oral instructions on Parting from the Four Attachments, the heart intent of the great, glorious Sakyapa, composed by Sakya Paṇḍita.

A Key to the Profound Essential Points

An Instruction Manual on the Mind Training of Parting from the Four Attachments

by Gorampa Sönam Senge

To those whose wisdom, like the sky, accommodates all things there are to know,
Whose compassion, like moonlight, beautifies the crowns of all beings,
Whose activities, like wish-granting gems, are treasures fulfilling all needs and wishes:
Matchless protector, lion of the Śākyas, who accomplishes perfect goodness for all beings;
Mañjughoṣa, who embodies the pristine wisdom of all victors of the three times;
Avalokiteśvara, who promised to protect all beings of the three realms;
And Sakyapa, who took human form to guide beings in these dark times;
To you, whose names are difficult to utter, I bow in devotion.

In reply to a repeated request made by someone with pure and wholesome intent,
Who, by the force of merit accumulated in the past has gained the support of a human body with which to practice the sublime Dharma,
And who, with spontaneously acquired wealth, supports the Dharma and its upholders,
I will now share uncommon instructions on the key points of the Mahāyāna.

The truly and perfectly awakened Buddha, who accomplishes the welfare of all worlds of existence without needing to be asked, taught a vast collection of Dharma in accordance with the dispositions, mentalities, and latent tendencies of those to be trained. All these teachings are gathered in the vehicle of the perfections and the vajra vehicle. The former is of two types: practice based mainly on explanations found in treatises and practice based on the key points given in pith instructions.

In terms of the practice based mainly on explanations from the treatises, the Protector Maitreya, in the *Ornament of Realization*, explains the stages of the path through eight sets of realization taught in the Perfection of Wisdom Sūtras,[1] and in the *Ornament of Mahāyāna Sūtras* he teaches that the intent of the sūtras of the Mahāyāna is conveyed through the subjects of spiritual potential, conviction in the Dharma, and so forth.[2]

In the *Precious Garland*, Ārya Nāgārjuna teaches the stages of the path in terms of two things to be accomplished—the higher realms and definite goodness (i.e., liberation)—and the means of accomplishing those, which are faith and wisdom.

Ācārya Āryadeva teaches the stages of the path by explaining that one first takes as one's aim buddhahood that has eliminated the four mistaken views,[3] and then cuts off afflictions along with their cause, which obstruct the accomplishment of bodhisattva deeds. Having become a suitable vessel for the realization of suchness, the main practice is then the nectar-like teaching of suchness.

Ācārya Śāntideva teaches the stages of the path to buddhahood, explaining that, with the support of a human body endowed with all freedoms and conducive conditions, one practices the six perfections, which are the essence of bodhisattva practice, conjoined with pure aspirations.

Jowo Atiśa teaches the stages of the path in terms of three types of individuals: individuals of lesser scope abandon attachment to this life and focus exclusively on the benefit of future lives; individuals of middling scope abandon the aim of happiness in saṃsāra and focus exclusively on liberation; and individuals of great scope accomplish buddhahood for the benefit of all beings.[4]

The glorious Candarkīrti teaches the stages of the path, explaining that at the level of an ordinary being, one practices compassion, bodhicitta, and the mind of non-duality, thereby attaining the state of an ārya. Then, one traverses the ten bhūmis through practicing the ten perfections, ultimately accomplishing the three kāyas.

The explanations by these accomplished masters elucidate the intent of the Mahāyāna scriptures in an unmistaken manner. Even though these excellent traditions are truly marvelous, they are to be understood by those who are well-trained in the scriptural tradition and cannot be learned here in a brief manner.

Second is the practice of the meaning of these traditions through the key points given in pith instructions. Even though, generally, there seem to be such teachings, there are mainly two traditions of pith instructions: those Lama Serlingpa gave to Jowo Atiśa and those the Protector Mañjughoṣa gave to Lama Sakyapa. In the first, one contemplates the difficulty of obtaining the freedoms and conducive conditions, death and impermanence, the law of karma – actions and their results, and the defects of saṃsāra. Through these four, one becomes a suitable vessel for the arising of bodhicitta. Then, having extensively trained in the preparatory practices of loving kindness and compassion, one engages in the main practice, which is primarily meditation on the bodhicitta of exchanging oneself for others. Occasionally, one also meditates on ultimate bodhicitta. The subsidiary practices of the path are: transforming unfavorable circumstances into the path of awakening, condensing everything into the practice of a single life, evaluating one's mind training, the commitments of mind training, and the precepts of mind training.

Practicing in this way, one has an extraordinary path that has little to show outwardly but yields great progress. In Tibet, Jowo Atiśa gave these teachings only to master Dromtönpa, who in turn gave them only to the three precious brothers.[5] From there, these teachings spread widely and became as renowned as the sun and moon in this land of snow mountains. For the practice of these teachings, one should look to the works of Gyalse Chödzongpa and his spiritual sons, as well as those of Sempa Chenpo Zhönnu Gyalchok and others.

Now, regarding the instructions the Protector Mañjughoṣa bestowed upon Lama Sakyapa, although the key points of practice are similar to those in the traditions mentioned above, this teaching is superior to others in terms of the phrasing of the subject matter and the sequence of meaning.

When Kunga Nyingpo, the great lama from Sakya, was twelve years old, he performed the practice of Mañjughoṣa. After six months he had a vision where Mañjughoṣa directly appeared to him and proclaimed:

If you are attached to this life, you are not a Dharma practitioner.
If you are attached to saṃsāra, you have no renunciation.
If you are attached to your own self-interest, you have no bodhicitta.
If there is grasping, it is not the view.

These lines encompass all the practices of the Pāramitāyāna. Their meaning consists of four aspects: parting from attachment to this life, one's mind turns to the Dharma; parting from attachment to saṃsāra, the Dharma becomes one's path; parting from attachment to self-interest, one eliminates confusion from the path; and parting from clinging to the four extremes, confusion dawns as pristine wisdom.

Parting from Attachment to this Life, One's Mind Turns to the Dharma

The practice based on the first line has three parts:
(1) preliminary, contemplating the difficulty of obtaining the freedoms and conducive conditions of a precious human life;
(2) main practice, contemplating death and impermanence; and
(3) subsidiary practice, contemplating the law of karma, actions and their results.

Contemplation on the Precious Human Life

Regarding the contemplation of the difficulty of obtaining the freedoms and conducive conditions: Sit comfortably and take refuge in the guru and Three Jewels many times. Then, make the supplication in four lines, praying for your mind to turn to the Dharma, etc. After this, generate bodhicitta, thinking "For the sake of all sentient beings, I must attain buddhahood, etc." Then, contemplate as follows:

"In terms of its nature, it is difficult to obtain a human body like the present one, complete with eight freedoms and ten conducive conditions. In terms of causes, it requires having accomplished wholesome deeds. Since there is hardly any wholesomeness in my mindstream, it is difficult to obtain such a life from this perspective as well. In terms of the odds, among the six realms, each lower realm has more beings than the higher ones. I can directly observe that the number of animals living in just one pond in the summertime, or in a pile of wood, exceeds all humans in the world. From this perspective I can also see that a precious human life is difficult to obtain. In terms of analogies, it is explained that it is more difficult to obtain a precious human birth than for a pea thrown against a wall to stick to it, or for a turtle in a storm-tossed ocean to insert its head into a floating wooden yoke. Therefore, having obtained freedoms and conducive conditions just this once, I must practice to benefit my future lives without wasting this opportunity." Contemplate in this way.

Contemplation of Death and Impermanence

After taking refuge and generating bodhicitta as before, contemplate as follows: "No one who is born remains alive forever without dying, so death is certain. Moreover, I have no confidence that I will die at a certain time and be alive until that point. There are many causes of death and few conditions for staying alive. I will certainly die. When the time of death arrives, nothing can prevent it – no medicine or rituals can help. After death, nothing except for Dharma will follow me, neither my present companions nor my worldly possessions." Meditating in this way will free you from attachment to this life.

This is the main method to bring the mind to the Dharma. Therefore, even when eating good food, wearing fine clothes, or surrounded by many companions, think: "Though I have these conditions now, someday I will have to leave them all and go alone. Therefore, these things are futile." Meditating in this way will free you from attachment to the activities of this life.

Contemplating the Law of Karma

Again, take refuge and generate bodhicitta as before. Then, contemplate as follows: "Having obtained these so difficult to find freedoms and conducive conditions, which are themselves impermanent, I must abandon all unwholesome actions and accomplish as many wholesome deeds as possible before I die.

The reason for this is as follows: The fully ripened result of committing the ten unwholesome actions is rebirth in the three lower realms. Such actions also produce two types of causally concordant results. The experience concordant with the cause includes a short life due to killing, poverty due to stealing, and so forth. The behavior concordant with the cause means that one will have the desire to engage in whatever unwholesome action one has become habituated to, leading once more to the result of descending to lower realms – thus leaving no opportunity for liberation. The environmental result is rebirth in places filled with foul odors and dust storms. Therefore, I must definitely abandon these actions." Contemplate in this way.

Likewise, contemplate: "The fully ripened result of the ten wholesome actions is rebirth in higher realms. Regarding the causally concordant results, the experience concordant with the cause includes a long life due to abandoning killing, and so forth. The behavior concordant with the cause is the desire to perform such wholesome actions again, and the environmental result is rebirth in places with pleasant fragrances, and so forth. Therefore, I must definitely accomplish these actions."

Most important here is to understand the key points about what to adopt and abandon in terms of actions and their results, and to act accordingly.

Parting from Attachment to Saṃsāra, the Dharma Becomes One's Path

To contemplate the defects of the three realms of saṃsāra, begin by taking refuge and generating bodhicitta as before. Then, proceed: "The nature of the three realms of saṃsāra is nothing but suffering. In the hot hells, beings endure sufferings of their bodies being burned by fire and cut by weapons. In the cold hells, they experience sufferings of such extreme cold that their flesh and bones split into pieces. In the neighboring hells, they suffer by dwelling in pits of burning embers. If even a fraction of these sufferings were to befall my present body, it would be unbearable. The hungry ghosts endure terrible sufferings of hunger, thirst, heat and cold, exhaustion, and fear. Animals living in the depths of the ocean suffer terribly from devouring each other, while animals scattered among humans suffer from being used and exploited.

Humans experience directly visible sufferings such as losing their status, seeking but not finding what they want, encountering what they don't want, being separated from loved ones, and so forth. Even the gods of the desire realm experience mental suffering that exceeds the physical suffering of hell beings, when signs of death and near-death appear. Although the gods of the form and formless realms do not experience manifest suffering in their present condition, they will eventually fall from their elevated state and experience again all the sufferings of the lower realms.

Therefore, the nature of the three realms of saṃsāra is nothing but suffering. That being so, I must abandon all of saṃsāra and attain the state of liberation." Contemplate in this way.

Up to this point, in terms of the stages of the path of the three types of individuals, this completes the paths of individuals of lesser and middling scope. According to Serlingpa's tradition, this completes the preliminaries, which are the four teachings that form the foundations of the path.

Parting from Attachment to Self-Interest, One Eliminates Confusion from the Path

This has three parts: cultivation of altruistic love, compassion, and bodhicitta.

Cultivation of Altruistic Love

"It is not enough to free oneself alone from the sufferings of saṃsāra. All beings throughout the three realms have been my kind parents countless times. My present mother, in particular, first carried me in her womb. After birth, when I was like a helpless worm, she protected my life. Then she cared for me with food, clothing, and so forth." Remembering all her kindness, contemplate: "My mother has been so kind to me. I must therefore establish her in happiness."

Then, contemplate how all other relatives and dear ones, even enemies who have harmed you, as well as those suffering in the three lower realms, and so forth, have all also been your mothers again and again since beginningless saṃsāra. Then, reflect on their kindness and repeatedly give rise to altruistic love in your mind, the wish to establish them in happiness.

Cultivation of Compassion

Remember all the kindness of your present mother and think: "Though my kind mother wants nothing more than to be free from suffering, the very nature of her present condition is nothing but suffering – this is so sad! If only she could be free from suffering! I shall establish her in freedom from suffering." Similarly, reflect on the kindness of all other beings as before and cultivate compassion, the wish for them to be free from suffering.

If these two—altruistic love and compassion—have not developed in one's mind, genuine bodhicitta will not arise. Since bodhicitta is the very root of all Mahāyāna dharmas, it is crucial to put great effort into these practices.

Cultivation of Bodhicitta

The cultivation of bodhicitta has three parts: aspirating bodhicitta, bodhicitta of equalizing oneself with others, and bodhicitta of exchanging oneself for others.

First, aspiring bodhicitta: "Though these kind parents of the three realms of saṃsāra want nothing but to be happy and to be free of suffering, I lack the power to accomplish this. Even powerful worldly beings like Brahma and Indra, and the śrāvakas and pratyekabuddhas who have transcended worldly existence do not have this power. Who can accomplish this? Only a truly and perfectly enlightened buddha has this power. Therefore, for the benefit of all beings, I must attain the state of complete awakening and liberate these kind parents from the ocean of saṃsāra." Cultivate the mind of bodhicitta by thinking in this way. It is the indispensable cause for attaining buddhahood. Because this mind transforms all wholesome deeds into causes for complete awakening, it is extensively praised in many Mahāyāna scriptures.

Second, the bodhicitta of equalizing oneself with others: "Just as I seek happiness, all beings seek happiness. Therefore, I shall work to accomplish the happiness of all beings, just as I work to accomplish my own. Just as I don't want to suffer, all beings don't wish to suffer. Therefore, I shall remove the suffering of all beings, just as I remove my own." Meditate in this way.

Third, the bodhicitta of exchanging oneself for others. Visualize your present mother before you and think: "Though my mother is so kind, the very nature of her present condition is nothing but suffering – this is so sad! May all her suffering along with its causes, unwholesome deeds, ripen upon me and may I experience them. May all my happiness and wholesome deeds ripen upon my mother and may she attain buddhahood." In the same way, cultivate bodhicitta by focusing on the following objects: other relatives and dear ones, people you have seen or heard about, enemies who have harmed you, those suffering in the lower realms, and so forth. Finally, think that the suffering of all beings collectively gathers upon yourself, and your happiness and wholesome deeds become whatever temporary enjoyments each being desires and ultimately the cause of their awakening.

This is the heart of the practice of the Mahāyāna, the secret instructions of all buddhas of the three times. Though the reasons why one should meditate like this, quotations from the scriptures, and clarification of doubts about the meditation method are important, I have not elaborated for fear of excessive length.

From aspiring bodhicitta up to this point, the preliminary practices of taking refuge and generating bodhicitta as previously taught are also definitely necessary. In addition, it is also good to practice guru yoga. At the conclusion of every meditation session, seal the practice with dedication prayers and aspirations. Moreover, maintain mindfulness during all activities of walking, moving about, lying down, and sitting.

Parting from Clinging to the Four Extremes, Confusion Dawns as Pristine Wisdom

Among the practices of calm abiding and special insight, other pith instruction traditions teach special insight through the meditations on selflessness of the individual and selflessness of phenomena, etc. In this tradition, however, special insight is cultivated during formal meditation sessions based on three topics: establishing appearances as mind, establishing mind as illusory, and establishing the illusory as devoid of inherent nature. For post-meditation, there is the practice of viewing things without clinging, like illusions and dreams. However, since meditating on these subjects on one's own without relying on a guru's instructions carries great risk of confusion, and since one cannot understand the meaning through words alone, I will not elaborate here.

That being said, the following words will be of immediate benefit. Whatever wholesome roots you accomplish, it is important that you don't develop conceit, seeing yourself as somebody who does good, your actions as good deeds, and therefore think: "I have performed these good deeds." There is no fault in stating without pride that you have performed a certain good action, if this is done to inspire others. And so, whenever you accomplish roots of goodness or engage in daily activities, if you remember to ask yourself questions like: "Is this an illusion? Is this a dream?" these actions become causes for understanding the view. Therefore, it is crucial to maintain mindfulness.

In this way, the path taught here has four stages: (1) by practicing for the benefit of future lives, the mind turns to the Dharma; (2) by abandoning saṃsāra and practicing the path to liberation, the Dharma becomes the path; (3) by abandoning the mindset of the Hīnayāna and engaging in Mahāyāna, one eliminates confusion from the path; and (4) by abandoning conceptual elaborations that grasp at extremes and engaging in the meaning of the fundamental nature, confusion dawns as pristine wisdom. Practice these most important points of the path, while making your daily activities meaningful. Make your body meaningful by making prostrations and circumambulations; make your speech meaningful by praising buddhas and bodhisattvas and reading profound sūtras; make your mind meaningful through meditating on altruistic love, compassion, and bodhicitta; and make your resources meaningful through making offerings to the Three Jewels and serving the Sangha. If these activities are conjoined with pure aspirations, you will definitely attain perfect buddhahood, free of flaws and endowed with all excellent qualities.

Verses summarizing these key points

The support of a human life with which to practice the sublime Dharma is difficult to obtain,
And, impermanent in nature, it perishes soon!
Understanding this well, adopting the wholesome and abandon the unwholesome,
Patiently striving in this way – this is the first stage.

Observing the endless stream of beings in this ocean of saṃsāra,
Caught in the jaws of the sea monster of suffering,
Generating renunciation, seeking the dry land of nirvāṇa's liberation –
This is the second stage.

All limitless beings have been your own father and mother, over and over again.
Remember their kindness, offering help and support.
With love, compassion, and supreme bodhicitta,
Accomplishing others' welfare – this is the third stage.

Having understood that whatever is perceived is but one's own mind;
That mind itself, like an illusion, is but a collection of causes and conditions;
And that the illusory is beyond conceptual elaboration;
Meditating on the fundamental nature – this is the fourth stage.

In all circumstances, by making offerings to the Three Jewels,
Gradually abandoning the unwholesome,
Helping those without protection and those in need through generosity,
And conjoining these with dedication of threefold purity,
Both temporary and ultimate benefit will certainly be accomplished.

This summary of the key points of the Mahāyāna path,
I offer to you, a patron of the teaching, as your heart practice,
With the intention that I may be of benefit.
Through its practice, may you accomplish all your aims.

This was written by the Buddhist monk Sönam Sengé at the sacred hermitage of Dokhar on the third day of the waxing moon in the month of Mindrug (3rd lunar), in response to a request from the lay bodhisattva Ralö Dorje, a noble patron of those who uphold the doctrine who has unwavering faith in the precious teaching, asking for words of advice, saying that he needed detailed instructions beneficial for practicing the divine Dharma. I will later present the essential points of the law of karma along with scriptural quotations. Maṅgalaṃ bhavantu! May it be auspicious!

Nectar from the Heart
A Song of Experience of Parting from the Four Attachments

by Jamyang Khyentse Wangpo

Through the blessings of Guru Mañjughoṣa,
May all beings throughout endless space engage in the sublime Dharma,
May they take Dharma as their path, pacify confusions on the path,
And may confused perception dawn as the ultimate expanse.

Though you may have obtained a support with freedoms and riches so difficult to gain,
If you are attached to this life, you are not a Dharma practitioner.
And so, since time passes every moment, and things are impermanent and bound to fall apart,
Strive in adopting what is wholesome and give up misdeeds.

Though you may have turned your mind toward the sublime Dharma,
If you are attached to the three realms, you have no renunciation.

And so, since saṃsāra is nothing but suffering in nature,
Generate genuine longing for liberation.

Though you may seek mere peace and happiness for yourself,
If you are attached to your own benefit, you have no bodhicitta.
And so, since all sentient beings are, in fact, your kind parents,
Cultivate love, compassion, and bodhicitta.

Though you may have trained in conventional bodhicitta,
If there is clinging, it is not the view.
To cut the root of the belief in a self,
Come to rest in the expanse beyond elaborations.

These words contain the essence of the instructions
Lord Mañjuśrī imparted to the Glorious and Compassionate master.
By the merit of composing this song with whatever experience came to mind,
May all mother sentient beings swiftly attain enlightenment.

Written by the carefree, aimlessly wandering yogi Jamyang Khyentse Wangpo in the Dharma center of glorious Sakya, the source of bountiful precious qualities, in the cave of Rangjung Dorje Drak. the very place where noble Mañjughoṣa directly appeared to the Great Sakyapa Lama and bestowed this teaching.
Sarva maṅgalam!

Khenchen Appey Rinpoche's Commentary

Outline of the Teaching

INTRODUCTORY TEACHINGS	29
I. Preliminary Advice	29
A. The Source of These Teachings	29
B. How to Approach Study and Practice	31
C. On the Practice of Meditation	32
D. Advice for Practice in Retreat	34
II. The Practice of Taking Refuge	35
A. The Causes for Taking Refuge	36
B. Identifying the Objects of Refuge	37
C. The Manner of Taking Refuge	40
1. Knowing the superior qualities of the Three Jewels	40
2. Understanding the distinguishing features of the Three Jewels	47
3. Acknowledging our commitment	48
4. Appreciating the difference to other objects of refuge	48
D. Practice Instructions	49
E. On the Vows, the Training, and Observances	52
F. The Benefits of Taking Refuge	55
III. On the Three Vehicles and the Five Paths	56

THE MAIN PART OF THE TEACHING ON PARTING
FROM THE FOUR ATTACHMENTS   59

A Summary of the Teaching   59
Four Attachments and Three Levels of Practice   61
A Commentary on the Supplication Prayer   62

THE FIRST LINE: "IF YOU ARE ATTACHED TO THIS LIFE,
YOU ARE NOT A DHARMA PRACTITIONER."   65

Introduction   65
I. The Freedoms and Conducive Conditions
   So Difficult to Obtain   67
  A. The Nature of a Precious Human Life   68
  B. The Causes for a Precious Human Life   69
  C. The Odds of Obtaining a Precious Human Life   70
  D. Analogies   70
II. Death and Impermanence   71
  A. Death is Certain   72
  B. The Time of Death is Uncertain   72
  C. Nothing Except for the Dharma Will Be of Help 73
III. Karma: Actions and Their Results   75
  A. Unwholesome Karma   76
    1. The ten unwholesome deeds   76
    2. Their results   80
    3. How to confess negative deeds by means of
      the four powers   82
  B. Wholesome Karma and its Results   83
  C. What Determines the Strength of Our Actions?   84

D. When Does Karma Ripen? 85
   E. Neutral Karma 86
IV. Dharma and One's Attachment to this Life 86
V. Drakpa Gyaltsen's Pith Instructions 88

THE SECOND LINE: "IF YOU ARE ATTACHED TO SAMSĀRA, YOU HAVE NO RENUNCIATION." 95

Introduction 95
I. A General Assessment of Samsāra 96
   A. The Three Categories of Suffering 96
   B. The Eight Types of Suffering 97
   C. The Six Types of Suffering 98
II. The Specific Sufferings of Sentient Beings 99
   A. The Suffering of Beings in the Hell Realm 99
   B. The Suffering of Hungry Ghosts 102
   C. The Suffering of Animals 103
   D. The Suffering of Humans 104
   E. The Suffering of the Gods 105
III. The Benefits of Contemplating the Suffering of Samsāra 106
IV. Supplementary Teachings 108
   A. Afflictions, Mind, and Mental Factors 108
   B. The Twelve Links of Dependent Arising 112
   C. Contemplating the Faults of the Afflictions 114
   D. The Wheel of Becoming 115

THE THIRD LINE: "IF YOU ARE ATTACHED TO
YOUR OWN SELF-INTEREST, YOU HAVE NO BODHICITTA." 117

Introduction 117

I. Cultivating Altruistic Love 118
   A. The Cause of Aspiring and Engaging Bodhicitta 118
   B. The Benefits of Cultivating Altruistic Love 119
   C. How to Cultivate Love 120
      1. Altruistic love for those close to us 120
         a. Love for our mother 121
            i. Thinking of one's mother 121
            ii. Recalling her great kindness 121
            iii. Wishing to repay her kindness 122
            iv. Four methods of practice 123
         b. Love for our dear ones 124
         c. Love for others with whom we have
            a good relation 124
      2. Love for enemies 124
      3. Love for all beings 125
      4. Training in post-meditation 125

II. Cultivating Compassion 126
   A. The Nature and the Benefits of Compassion 126
   B. How to Cultivate Compassion 127

III. Bodhicitta 130
   A. Aspiring Bodhicitta and Its Benefits 131
   B. The Bodhicitta Vow and the Training 133
      1. The training for individuals of lesser capacity 135
      2. The training for individuals of middling capacity 136
      3. The training for individuals of highest capacity 137

C. The Bodhicitta Practice of Equalizing Oneself
with Others 137
D. Tonglen, the Practice of Exchanging Oneself
for Others 140
   1. The nature and practice of tonglen 140
   2. On the benefits of exchanging oneself for others 143
E. The Six Perfections 146
   1. The nature of the perfections 146
   2. The perfection of generosity 146
      a. The nature of generosity 146
      b. Three forms of generosity and
         the right preparation 148
      c. The actual act of giving 150
      d. How to correctly accomplish the perfection of
         generosity 151
   3. The beneficial results of the perfections 153

THE FOURTH LINE: "IF THERE IS GRASPING,
IT IS NOT THE VIEW." 155

Introduction 155

I. The Perfection of Meditation 156
  A. Why Meditate? 156
  B. The Prerequisites for Samādhi 157
  C. The Actual Practice of Meditation 159
    1. Preliminary reflections and prayers 159
    2. The object of meditation 160
    3. The posture 161

4. Nine methods to settle the mind   162
   a. Placing the mind   162
   b. The five hindrances and their eight antidotes   163
   c. The remaining eight methods to settle the mind   166
5. Worldly calm abiding and beyond   168
6. Some practical instructions   169

II. The Perfection of Wisdom   171
  A. What is Wisdom?   171
  B. How is Wisdom Cultivated?   173
  C. The Dangers of Teaching "Emptiness"   173
  D. Approaches to Selflessness and the Two Realities   174
  E. The Two Types of Selflessness   175
    1. The self of the individual   176
      a. Searching for the self   176
      b. Applying the view in meditation   177
      c. The self and the five skandhas   178
    2. The self of phenomena   180
      a. Examining phenomena by means of reasoning   180
      b. Emptiness beyond nonexistence   182
  F. Pith Instructions for Insight   184
    1. Establishing appearances as mind   185
    2. Establishing mind as illusory   185
    3. Establishing the illusory as devoid of inherent nature   186

CONCLUDING WORDS OF ADVICE   187

Introductory Teachings

I. Preliminary Advice

A. The Source of These Teachings

To study these teachings, I request you to generate the following motivation: "In order to benefit all sentient beings I must attain buddhahood. For this purpose, I shall study the Dharma and reflect upon these teachings."

I am very pleased to see so many people who have come here from afar with great interest in the Dharma. During this course, we are going to study the teaching known as *Parting from the Four Attachments*.

Generally speaking, the Buddha's teachings can be divided into three categories: first, the sūtras, which are the words spoken by the Buddha; second, the śāstras or treatises, composed by great scholars from India and other places, which expound on the Buddha's intent; and third, the pith instructions, which mainly present a gradual approach for beginners on how to practice the various paths to higher rebirth and liberation taught in the sūtras and śāstras.

In Tibet, many Mahāyāna pith instructions were transmitted that belong neither to the vehicle of the śrāvakas nor to the path of Secret Mantra. Among these, the two most famous ones are the lojong mind training teachings given by Serlingpa to Jowo

Jé Palden Atiśa and the pith instructions on *Parting from the Four Attachments*, which the noble Mañjughoṣa imparted on Sachen Kunga Nyingpo.

The greatness of Mañjughoṣa is described in many sūtras. It is said, for instance, that uttering the name of a single buddha accrues great merit, let alone the merit generated by pronouncing the names of many buddhas. But whoever calls the name of Mañjughoṣa just once will produce merit even greater than that of reciting for eons the names of buddhas equal in number to the grains of sand on the banks of the river Ganges. The reason for this is that Mañjughoṣa carries out the enlightened activities of all the buddhas. In fact, the buddha of our time, as well as many other buddhas, first generated bodhicitta—the resolve to attain supreme awakening—because of Mañjughoṣa, and it was also he who incited them to engage in the practices of the path. This is one reason why Mañjughoṣa is said to be the father of all buddhas. Another reason is that the actual or ultimate Mañjughoṣa is the wisdom mind of all the buddhas. The noble protector Maitreya stated: "Even if many bodhisattvas of the tenth bhūmi, like myself, were to observe him with great attention, we would still not be able to comprehend even the way Mañjughoṣa moves about." The sūtras contain many such stories illustrating the amazing qualities of this bodhisattva.

Several commentaries are used for the study of the instructions of *Parting from the Four Attachments*. Of these, I will mainly rely on the text by Künkhyen Gorampa Sönam Sengé. Please refer to this text and also consult other commentaries. The content of the teachings covers the stages of the path according to the Pāramitāyāna, which are also explained in works such as Ngorchen Könchok Lhundrup's *Ornament to Beautify the Three Appearances*, Sakya Paṇḍita's *Clarifying the Sage's Intent*, and Müchen Sempa Chenpo's teachings on mind training. These texts only differ slightly in terms of the structure in which they organize the teachings.

B. How to Approach Study and Practice

I have nothing to explain that comes from my personal experience gained through meditation, nor do I have any advice for you that you cannot find elsewhere. Nevertheless, since most of the students who came here from abroad with great faith in the Buddhadharma have not had the opportunity to study the great treatises, I will speak a little about the qualities of the Three Jewels and about the Mahāyāna teachings. In this way I hope to plant some seeds of the Mahāyāna Dharma in your minds.

Throughout this course, we will engage in both study and practice. Since we plan to study, reflect, and meditate, we should organize our time well. Besides attending the main classes, we should also engage in self-study and practice. If you set aside one and a half hours every day for your personal studies, you could use the first forty-five minutes to read the texts and reflect upon their meaning and the remaining time to meditate. Alternatively, it is also good to devote one entire session to study and another to meditation.

We should approach every line of the Buddha's teachings in this way: learn them, reflect on the meaning, and cultivate it through meditation. In this way, the three wisdoms will arise. The wisdom that arises from listening is the knowledge we acquire from our teacher or by studying the scriptures composed by genuine masters. Once we have acquired this type of wisdom, we must investigate. Using our own intelligence and reasoning, we analyze the meaning of the teachings we have learned to strengthen and stabilize our understanding. The knowledge gained in this way is called the wisdom that arises from contemplation.

When teaching the Dharma to others, it is often not possible to determine with certainty the definitive meaning of a given passage. In such cases it is acceptable and indeed skillful to state that different masters explain certain points in different ways. In the context of practice, however, one should not have this approach: one needs to settle on one point. Imagine someone traveling along an unknown road. At one point he reaches a junction and there are only two ways to go forward: left or right. A choice must be made since it is impossible to continue on both roads. It is the same in our practice: we must first reach certainty with whatever it is we are cultivating and then familiarize ourselves with it by recollecting it over and over again. This is the meaning of meditation or practice.

C. On the Practice of Meditation

There are two types of meditative cultivation: calm abiding or *śamatha*, and special insight or *vipaśyanā*. By cultivating calm abiding through the practice of meditative absorption, we develop stability of mind. Whatever we cultivate on the basis of this mind, whether it is loving-kindness, compassion, or any other wholesome state, we will quickly see the results of our efforts and our minds will develop accordingly. The mastery of calm abiding is indispensable to accomplish the higher paths of the three vehicles. However, even those who have not achieved calm abiding can have a direct realization of death and impermanence and give rise to genuine loving-kindness and compassion, etc. if they repeatedly cultivate these contemplations with single-pointed concentration.

There are two methods of meditation: analytical meditation and placement meditation. To practice calm abiding, we cultivate attention by focusing the mind over and over again exclusively on the object of meditation, avoiding any distraction. This does not require any analysis.

In contrast, both analytical and placement meditation are required for the practice of special insight. When we meditate on the topic of no-self, for instance, we do so by first contemplating one or more reasons that establish the nonexistence of the self. Having cleared all doubts and misconceptions, we then place the mind one-pointedly on the view we have established in this way. This is the process of analytical meditation. Once we have gained certainty and are familiar with the process of establishing the view, it is no longer necessary to go through these lines of reasoning over and over again. Instead, we can directly focus on the view of selflessness established thus and familiarize the mind with it in this way. This is what is known as placement meditation.

The same applies to other practices as well. For the cultivation of compassion, for example, we use certain contemplations that function as the cause for generating compassion towards all sentient beings. We think about how all sentient beings have been our mothers in previous lives, that they are now experiencing tremendous suffering, and so on. These are forms of analytical meditation. When we cultivate compassion without the support of these contemplations, but instead simply think "Oh my! All beings truly deserve compassion!" and continually place our mind on this thought, it is called placement meditation. We can do this by repeating "May all sentient beings be free from suffering and the causes of suffering" one hundred times with the help of our mālā, recollecting the meaning of these words with each bead passing through our fingers. To practice in this way is very effective. These general remarks can be applied to any topic of meditation.

D. General Advice for Practice in Retreat

It is important that you use the entire duration of the course to engage in wholesome deeds. This can be accomplished in many different ways. In the Secret Mantra, a wide variety of yogic practices are taught, such as the yoga of eating, the yogas of conduct and so forth, but we also find similar practices in the Pāramitāyāna. For instance, when going to sleep you should think, "May all sentient beings obtain the dharmakāya of buddhahood." This does not mean that our sleep state is the dharmakāya, but by creating this connection based on their similarities and making the appropriate aspiration, our sleep becomes wholesome. On waking up, think, "May all sentient beings awake from the sleep of ignorance." As you get up, generate the thought "May they obtain the rūpakaya." While putting on your clothes, think, "May all wear the garments of shame and consideration." When washing, think, "May I wash away the stains of the afflictions." These are just a few examples of the phrases we can use. These words and their meanings, which are found in the sūtras and śāstras—the discourses of the Buddha and the treatises by the great masters—should be memorized. If you are able to recall them at the right time, your neutral actions will become virtuous. While eating, think, "May all beings obtain the nourishment of samādhi." Similarly, while eating or drinking dwell on the thought "May all the organisms living within my body be satiated with this food, and may they later be nourished by the true Dharma." By changing our motivation in this way, the action of eating becomes virtuous.

To engage in serious meditation practice, we must first possess the basis of ethical discipline and cut through all doubts and misconceptions by hearing and reflection. Then, we should retreat to practice in isolation. There are two types of isolation:

isolation of body and isolation of mind. To dwell in solitude away from other people is the isolation of the body. To relinquish the thoughts of desire and attachment towards beings and possessions is the isolation of the mind. If we rely on these two types of solitude, single-pointed meditation will quickly bring about results. Conversely, if we continue mingling with others and going about our usual business, the practice will not be very effective even if we meditate for a long time.

During these ten days of meditation practice, you all have your own room. Close the door to your room. If you also close the door to your discursive thoughts, both isolation of body and isolation of mind will be achieved. When we engage in meditation, we should not push ourselves too much; there should not be any hardships of body and mind. Be sure to get enough rest; the body must be relaxed. And do not talk a lot. Do not recite many prayers. Do not burden your mind with work. It is important to be at ease.

In terms of sleep, it is not beneficial to sleep during the daytime. Doing so is a mistake. You should sleep at night: that is the best kind of sleep, the most refreshing. Also, it is best not to talk much after the evening session: talk only when it is necessary, otherwise it is better not to speak. That is also part of the Mahāyāna teachings which we must put into practice.

II. The Practice of Taking Refuge

Taking refuge is the foundation for all practices and the door to all Dharma teachings. Why do we use the phrase "to take refuge"? When we are in danger and are unable to overcome the situation by ourselves, we seek protection with someone who is able to help us, similar to finding shelter from the rain under an overhanging rock. We call that helper our refuge.

What are the dangers we are facing in saṃsāra? Since beginningless time and over the course of countless lives, we have continuously experienced so many dangers and so much harm and suffering in saṃsāra. Even if we have now entered the path of liberation, if we do not bring about any true change within, this will go on and there will be no end to our plight. As Śāntideva explained, when we take birth in hell we will think, "Where can I find someone to help me, someone to save me from this terror?" We can look in the four directions but nowhere will we find anyone able to help us at that time. There will be no refuge. Therefore, now that we have the freedom to do so we should take refuge, starting from today.

A. The Causes for Taking Refuge

At this moment our mindstream carries many complete causes for rebirth in the lower realms. To prevent this from happening, we need a condition obstructing such a rebirth, which is the genuine Dharma. However, it is unlikely at this point that we possess such Dharma in our mindstream. Therefore, for ninety-nine per cent of people dying, this means that they risk being reborn in the lower realms, including the hell realms. Our situation is therefore extremely volatile and holds a great many dangers. Therefore, fear is the first cause for taking refuge.

The second cause for taking refuge is faith or conviction. There are three kinds of faith: clear faith, aspiring faith, and trusting faith. Clear faith can be compared to clear water. Just like clear water is not turbid with mud, clear faith is a mind free of the turbidity of doubt and lack of trust that admires the great qualities of the Three Jewels. Aspiring faith is the wish to attain those great qualities. Trusting faith is the thought that by taking refuge in the Three Jewels and relying on them, one will be protected from all fears and will not be deceived.

Another cause for taking refuge is compassion. The Mahāyāna path and its result come about due to compassion. This means that without compassion, there is no authentic Mahāyāna path. Since the goal of the Hīnayāna is to accomplish one's own benefit, for this path there are only two causes for refuge: fear and faith. When we go for refuge in accordance with the Mahāyāna we do so for the benefit of others. Therefore, compassion—the wish for all sentient beings to be free from suffering—is a third cause of taking refuge for those who follow the Mahāyāna.

B. *Identifying the Objects of Refuge*

The objects of refuge are the Three Jewels: Buddha, Dharma, and Sangha. From the perspective of the Hīnayāna, the term *Buddha* refers to the form body, or rūpakāya, of the Buddha. *Dharma* refers to the Hīnayāna Dharma, and *Sangha* to the eight types of ārya beings of the Hīnayāna.[1]

According to the Māhayāna tradition, *Buddha* refers to the three kāyas, or bodies of awakening. Someone who has not studied the scriptures might misunderstand this to indicate three individuals. This is not the case. When someone reaches buddhahood, one attains the three kāyas. The actual buddha is the saṃbhogakāya, or body of perfect enjoyment. It abides in a pure buddha realm where it teaches the Dharma in a bodily form seen only by a retinue of ārya bodhisattvas. Second is the dharmakāya, or Dharma body, which is the wisdom mind of that buddha. And lastly, the nirmāṇakāya, or emanation body, is the form emanated by the saṃbhogakāya to benefit sentient beings, regardless of the level of their faculties. The nirmāṇakāya can manifest as a bodhisattva, a śrāvaka, a pratyekabuddha, or as an ordinary being. It can appear a friend or an enemy, as someone who is pleasant to listen to or as someone unpleasant. It can take the form of a wealthy person or of someone very poor, of a highly respected individual or of someone who is despised by others. It also can appear in the form of inanimate objects such as a boat, a bridge, or so forth. The nirmāṇakāya will also convey different kinds of Dharma teachings in accordance with the inclinations and needs of those to be taught.

The Dharma Jewel is the Mahāyāna Dharma, which can be divided into the Dharma of transmission and the Dharma of realization. In simple terms, the Dharma of transmission is the words of the Buddha. The Buddha spoke these words a long time ago, and they remained in the mindstreams of the bodhisattvas. Now they are found in the volumes of the scriptures. The Dharma of realization encompasses two aspects: cessation and path. *Cessation* refers to the truth of cessation, which is the true nature of the mind of the ārya bodhisattvas, the freedom from stains attained through the power of the path. *Path* refers to the antidotes that eliminate the afflictions: the wisdom, compassion, and so forth present in the mindstream of the ārya bodhisattvas. This is the truth of the path.

In brief, the Dharma Jewel, as an object of refuge, comprises the truth of cessation and the truth of the path present in the mindstreams of the bodhisattvas on the ten bhūmis. Even though cessation and path are present in the continuum of the buddhas as well, they are referred to as the dharmakāya in this case, which means that they are included in the Buddha Jewel.

The Sangha Jewel refers to the bodhisattvas who dwell on the ten bhūmis or grounds. These are the Three Jewels that are our objects of refuge.

One might ask, "How many buddhas are there, and do we have to go to all of them for refuge?" We can say that there are infinite buddhas. Just as the sky is boundless and the number of sentient beings is limitless, the Buddhas, the Dharma, and the

Sangha are all limitless as well. However, the Buddha as the object of refuge includes all buddhas. This means that when we seek refuge with just one buddha, Śākyamuni Buddha for example, we in fact take refuge in all the buddhas. There is no difference between going for refuge to one and to many buddhas.

You might wonder, why can only the Three Jewels be our objects of refuge? To take an example, if we have seriously violated the law and are not able to solve our problems and dispel our fears on our own, we must seek help from someone else. That person should be knowledgeable about the situation, be willing to help, and have the ability to do so. They must have all three of these characteristics. Similarly, the buddhas and bodhisattvas possess all three of these qualities: knowledge, compassion, and ability. Since only the Three Jewels perfectly possess these qualities, we seek protection with them.

In response to this question, Ārya Asaṅga stated that objects of refuge must possess four qualities. First, they must themselves be completely free from all that we seek protection from. For example, if you see another person drowning in a torrent while you yourself are also being carried away by the water, you will not be able to save them. Secondly, objects of refuge must be skilled in the methods for liberating sentient beings. Thirdly, they must be endowed with compassion. And fourthly, they must not require any compensation. If it is necessary to reward someone in order to receive their help, it becomes difficult to find help. The buddhas and bodhisattvas, on the other hand, extend their help regardless of whether others revere or harm them, and they also help those who do not even engage with them. Since only the Three Jewels possess these four qualities completely, they alone are our objects of refuge.

C. The Manner of Taking Refuge

To take refuge in the Three Jewels means that we resolve to rely on the Buddha as our teacher, the Dharma as our path to liberation, and the Sangha as our companions to help us accomplish the path. To take refuge, then, is first and foremost a mental activity as opposed to merely saying the words "I go for refuge," which is a verbal activity.

Ārya Asaṅga explained that certain features are required to qualify our practice of taking refuge as genuine. First, we should know the qualities of the Three Jewels well. Second, we should understand their distinguishing features. Third, we should know what we are committing to when we take refuge in them. And fourth, we should understand how our taking refuge in the Three Jewels excludes other objects of refuge. In other words, once we understand the differences between our own objects of refuge and those of other traditions, we should solely rely on the Three Jewels.

1. Knowing the superior qualities of the Three Jewels

The qualities of the Buddha

Since it is essential to know the qualities of the Three Jewels, I will explain them briefly. When speaking of the Buddha, we refer to someone who is free from all faults and who possesses all sublime qualities. Especially when he teaches others, the Buddha makes no mistakes whatsoever. These are, in short, the qualities of the Buddha.

In terms of the qualities of his speech, the Buddha's voice possesses sixty-four qualities: it is soft, pleasant, far-resounding, and so on. Not only is the Dharma heard throughout limitless world systems in this way, but the different listeners will all hear the Dharma expounded in their own tongue. Furthermore, the same speech of the Buddha will be received in different ways by individual disciples. For instance, some will hear the Buddha teach the path towards higher rebirth and others will hear him teach the paths of the three vehicles. In this way it occurred that three different disciples heard three different sūtras on the same occasion. These can now be found in the Kangyur, the collection of translated words of the Buddha.

The mind of the Buddha is replete with undefiled qualities, which are divided into twenty-one categories. We will talk about two of these, namely the Buddha's wisdom and the Buddha's compassion.

Through his wisdom the Buddha directly sees all objects of knowledge in one instant, just as we see the visible objects that are right in front of us. He also directly perceives the true nature of all phenomena. All beings who are not buddhas possess limited knowledge; there are always things they are unable to know. Even the bodhisattvas who abide on the tenth bodhisattva ground cannot know all things—not to mention the gods and other worldly beings—nor do they fully realize the ultimate nature of phenomena. The wisdom of the Buddha, however, extends to all objects of knowledge without exception. It is due to this omniscient wisdom that the Buddha is the teacher of all beings, including the gods.

In terms of his compassion, the Buddha cultivated for many uncountable eons the altruistic intention to liberate all limitless sentient beings from the dangers and faults of saṃsāra and nirvāṇa. Due to this, his mind has completely transformed into the nature of compassion and so he now caringly watches over all sentient beings at all times. In short, we can say that the Buddha's qualities are limitless. This being so, however many qualities of the Buddha one might mention, there will always be more to explain and their number will never diminish.

What are the causes of the Buddha's qualities? Their root is compassion and the cause is bodhicitta, the mind of enlightenment. The conditions for perfecting them are the methods of generosity, ethical discipline and so forth. Their ultimate result arises from having cultivated, for a long time, the intention to benefit and accomplish the welfare of sentient beings along with the immeasurable activities motivated by this intention. Thus, the causes of buddhahood are perfectly complete.

Perfect enlightened activity

The term *enlightened activity* refers to a buddha's deeds. Since the buddhas have completely achieved their own welfare through perfect awakening, they do not carry out any actions for this purpose. Whatever they do is for the benefit of others.

A buddha's enlightened activity has many subdivisions. First, a buddha accomplishes a variety of enlightened deeds. This refers to the many approaches and types of activity used to tame sentient beings. Even though the main activity is teaching the Dharma, they also engage in many other types of deeds. In *Entering the Middle Way*, Ācārya Candrakīrti stated that a buddha performs more activities in one instant than the number of grains of sand in the world.

Second, his activity is said to pervade. This means that the Buddha's enlightened activity reaches all those to be tamed, wherever they might be. Third, his deeds are spontaneously accomplished, which means that the Buddha naturally engages in and accomplishes his activities, without any effort and without having to generate the thought to engage in any particular deed. His activity is also always timely. This means that the Buddha is able to act perfectly whenever it is needed; he never does anything too early or too late. Fifth, the activity is uninterrupted, which means that the Buddha continuously performs enlightened activity without ever taking any break. Sixth, it is continuous: the Buddha will accomplish the benefit of beings as long as cyclic existence remains. His enlightened activity will not end before all sentient beings have attained the state of buddhahood. Since there will never be a time when there will be no more sentient beings, it is impossible for there to be a time without the enlightened activity of the Buddha.

The extent of his activity

The distinguishing characteristic of the Buddha's enlightened activity is that every single deed is performed solely for the welfare of others, including the simple act of breathing and the four types of physical posture (i.e., standing, walking, sitting, and lying down). With each light ray emanated from his body and every Dharma teaching he gave, the Buddha placed myriads of beings on the paths towards the two types of higher rebirth, the four stages of realization on the path of śrāvakas—such as stream-enterer and so forth—and on the Mahāyāna path. Even after the Buddha had manifested passing into parinirvāṇa, the seed of liberation is still planted in many beings by means of the representations of his body, his relics, stūpas, and the places where he performed his activities. Of particular significance are the scriptures containing the Buddha's words, since these teach the path of liberation. If a person educated in the Dharma prostrates before an image of the Buddha with faith and motivated by bodhicitta, this deed is obviously very meritorious. But even when someone who does not know anything about the Dharma happens to stumble upon an image of the Buddha or inadvertently walks around a stūpa, that person will ultimately attain enlightenment, because they will have created a connection with the unsurpassable merit field of the buddhas by encountering their representations.

The qualities of the Dharma

As sentient beings we are all engaged in some work or activity. The aim is always to obtain happiness and to be free from suffering. The Dharma is the only means that enables us to achieve this aim completely. No other method can accomplish this. Śāntideva explained that the true Dharma is the medicine that cures all suffering and the source of all happiness. This is the underlying purpose of all the teachings and practices of both the greater and the lesser vehicle. The Mahāyāna Dharma in particular is said to have inconceivable qualities that enable the practitioners to achieve the state of buddhahood. Thus, by contemplating the result, we can understand the greatness of the Mahāyāna Dharma.

Explained in brief, the Mahāyāna Dharma comprises two aspects: method and wisdom. The method consists of the activities that accomplish the benefit of others based on compassion, such as the practice of generosity. Wisdom is the knowledge that realizes the ultimate nature of things. The method aspect is able to bring about the qualities of a buddha, and the wisdom aspect has the capacity to dispel all faults without exception. The method comprises aspects such as compassion, loving-kindness, generosity, and so forth, all of which have many incredible benefits. These benefits are also the qualities of the Dharma.

The qualities of the Sangha

All Sangha of both the greater and the lesser vehicle engage in the three higher trainings. For this reason, the sūtra entitled *Recalling the Three Jewels* states, "They engaged excellently.

They engaged insightfully." As a result, the sūtra further states that they are worthy of homage and worthy of offerings by other sentient beings. Especially ārya bodhisattvas have inconceivable qualities. When they reach the first bhūmi, they obtain a treasury of many qualities. At this point they are free from all afflictions, suffering, and fear, but they still have much to accomplish to achieve buddhahood. Their two main activities are to gather the two accumulations and to accomplish the benefit of sentient beings. However, ārya bodhisattvas face no hardships in the pursuit of their aims. When they reach the first bhūmi, they are able to emanate one hundred bodies at the same time, on the second ground one thousand, on the third ground ten thousand, and so forth. With these bodies they can visit the buddha fields, stay in the presence of many buddhas, receive their teachings, and contemplate them. They do not lack in resources to make material offerings to the buddhas since their previous practice of generosity has provided them with many riches. And by the power of their samādhi they can further emanate vast offerings. When bodhisattvas invite the Buddha together with his retinue, they are able to present them with vast offerings, which they emanate by the power of their samādhi. Such offerings include baldachins, victory banners, accommodation, seats, plates and food, robes to be gifted to the monastic community, and so forth. These offerings are unsurpassed because their cause is the bodhisattva's samādhi, rather than karma and afflictions.

For example, when a bodhisattva offers a single material flower, they can at the same time emanate vast flower offerings through their samādhi. Some will be in the form of canopies in the sky, some palaces, umbrellas and victory banners, flower garlands to be offered to the guests, petals to cover the ground, and so forth. Having filled the whole of space in this way, everything is offered. In the same way, they emanate many other offerings, such as incense, lights, food, and so forth. The bodhisattvas are able to do so because they have realized the fact that all notions of size and quantity are merely created by the mind. Concepts of "large" and "small", "many" and "few" are not truly established in reality. Those who have attained direct cognition of reality are thereby able to transform small things into great ones and change few items into many. Furthermore, time is also just a mental perception. Those who see reality as it is have realized that there is no real "short" or "long" time, and are therefore able to gather the accumulations that take many eons to complete in the shortest time.

Since we are not able to do this ourselves at this point, we should imagine it and train our minds in this way. Suppose you are making a flower offering to the Buddha. Even if it is just an ordinary flower, think of it as the most beautiful one. If you only have a few small flowers, multiply them mentally and imagine that you are offering vast flower arrangements. This approach can be taken even further. When you make a maṇḍala offering, for example, think to yourself that by offering it once you are completing the accumulations, which takes eons to complete. If we now train in this by means of our imagination, we will later be able to gather the accumulations in this way once we have reached the bhūmis.

Ārya bodhisattvas possess what is called the samādhi of the treasury of space. With this samādhi they can transform the sky into a treasury of riches. With a simple wave of the hand, these bodhisattvas draw from space whatever they require to benefit sentient beings, as if it came from the sky. They are also able to emanate one hundred thousand bodies at once to work for the welfare of many sentient beings. Bodhisattvas accomplish the benefit of sentient beings in so many ways. Their main activities, however, are to explain the Dharma so that others know the paths to liberation and to omniscience, and to help them engage in the practice.

These highly realized bodhisattvas have heard many teachings directly from the buddhas and they understand the meaning of their words by themselves without having to rely on another teacher. They are therefore able to explain myriads of Dharma teachings, and they can do so simultaneously by means of a multitude of emanated bodies. They can also radiate light from their bodies. With one ray of light they eliminate the suffering of beings in the lower realms, and with another they inspire goodness in the minds of sentient beings. In this way, they accomplish all kinds of benefit for beings with the light they emanate. These are just some of the inconceivable enlightened activities of bodhisattvas.

In brief, we can say that the Buddha, Dharma, and Sangha possess inconceivable qualities.

2. Understanding the distinguishing features of the Three Jewels

We will now discuss the distinguishing features of each of the Three Jewels. The term *Buddha* refers to the state of awakening, *Dharma* to the result born from that awakening, and *Sangha* to those who practice that Dharma. The most important thing to understand in this regard is how the Three Jewels protect us from suffering. The Buddha proclaimed the Dharma, teaching us the paths to higher rebirth and liberation. This is how the Buddha protects his followers temporarily from bad migrations and ultimately from all the suffering and fear of saṃsāra: by teaching the Dharma, which, if we ourselves apply it and put it into practice, has the ability to gradually protect us from suffering.

How does the Dharma protect us? The Dharma of realization that is present in the mindstream of the noble Sangha, like Mañjughoṣa, cannot directly save us. However, if we practice in accordance with the Dharma taught by the Buddha, our own practice will eradicate the root of suffering, that is self-grasping and the mental afflictions, in our mind. This is how we will be protected from suffering.

The Sangha protects us by supporting us on this path. They encourage and inspire us to practice the Dharma and praise us when we do so. In this way, they spur our interest and enthusiasm to engage in Dharma practice.

3. Acknowledging our commitment

The third point Ārya Asaṅga mentioned to ensure that our practice of taking refuge is genuine is easy to understand: What are we promising in relation to each of the Three Jewels? We accept the Buddha as our teacher, the Dharma as our path, and the Sangha as the companions to help us accomplish the true Dharma. It is with this attitude that we go for refuge to the Three Jewels.

4. Appreciating the difference to other objects of refuge

What is the difference between the Three Jewels and the objects of refuge in other traditions? Why are we instructed to seek refuge only with the Three Jewels? Since Hindu gods like Brahmā and Viṣṇu, as well as their great saints, have not overcome all mental afflictions, the suffering that afflicts beings in saṃsāra is bound to reoccur for them. We can therefore not be freed from all suffering and fear by relying on them. Furthermore, their teachings also contain contradictory claims about these gods. For instance, Iśvara, their supreme god, is said to be permanent and the creator of the world and all beings. However, the term *permanent* means that he should be completely unmoving, implying that he could not accomplish any work. This is an example of a contradiction in their teaching.

In terms of their doctrine, certain traditions teach that liberation is attained by bathing in one of their great rivers, others maintain that it is granted by their supreme god, and others believe that it is obtained by knowing the twenty-five aspects of reality.[2] However, liberation cannot be attained by following these paths. Why is this so? The root of saṃsāra is self-grasping. To eradicate this view, we require the cognition of the nonexistence of the self. Without this wisdom, it is impossible to uproot self-grasping. This means that the paths that do not eliminate this mistaken view cannot free us from saṃsāra. All the various schools of Hindu thought maintain the existence of the self and they view the assertion of no-self as the main fault of the Buddhist tradition. From their perspective, Buddhism is a nihilistic tradition.

The followers of these teachings exert themselves in ascetic practices that are incapable of producing the results they strive for, and they take great pride in their doctrine and practice.

D. Practice Instructions[3]

Before you sit down, start by cleaning your room. If you can, arrange a shrine with a statue of the Buddha, a scripture containing his words, and a stūpa. If possible, also prepare offerings such as water, flowers, incense, and so forth in front of these representations. These offerings should be clean in the sense that they are untainted by negative deeds. Then sit down on a comfortable seat in the appropriate posture for meditation. Relax your body and your mind; be at ease.

Then, visualize Buddha Śākyamuni in the space in front of you, surrounded by the buddhas and bodhisattvas of the ten directions. Although all buddhas are equal in terms of their qualities, we visualize Buddha Śākyamuni as the principal figure in front of us because he is the buddha of our time and the teacher of the doctrine we are following. We imagine all these buddhas and bodhisattvas to be truly in front of us. In a way it is like a blind person knowing that a seeing person is in front of them. Do not visualize them sitting tightly together but imagine each of them sitting spaciously on their own throne with offerings in front of them, surrounded by their retinue.

Then, think of those who go for refuge, namely yourself, surrounded to all sides by all sentient beings, all in the form of human beings. Then recite the refuge prayer. When saying "I" think of yourself, and with "and all sentient beings" think of all sentient beings going for refuge. Since, according to the Mahāyāna tradition, we go for refuge together with all sentient beings, we should not recite "I go for refuge", but rather "We go for refuge." If not, our recitation becomes that of the lesser vehicle, not the Mahāyāna.

"From now until we reach enlightenment" defines the timespan. The followers of the Hīnayāna tradition would say "I take refuge until I die," but in accord with the Mahāyāna tradition we recite "we take refuge until we reach awakening." This indicates the duration of our practice.

When saying "We go for refuge to the Buddha" think of the Buddha as the teacher. When reciting "We go for refuge to the Dharma" think of the Dharma as the path, and with "We go for refuge to the Sangha" think of the Sangha as our companions on the path. Think that the Three Jewels are our true and infallible objects of refuge since they have the qualities of love, wisdom, and power, and the four distinguishing characteristics of an object of refuge.

To strengthen our motivation, we should think in the following way: "I and all sentient beings are subject to unbearable sufferings and endless fears. In our pitiable state, we are deserving objects of the buddhas' compassion. However, until now we never put our trust in the Three Jewels and failed to accept their intent. We have been trying to solve our problems by ourselves in so many ways and struggled so much. What do we have to show for it? Nothing but suffering and dissatisfaction. We shall therefore now seek refuge in the Three Jewels." Whatever we go through, highs or lows, happiness or misery, whatever happens we should trust that the Three Jewels know and understand. And we do not need to be reluctant. We should trust them wholeheartedly and take refuge in the Buddha, the Dharma, and the Sangha with complete confidence. If, on our side, we act in accordance with the Buddha's advice and sincerely trust that the Triple Gem knows, all causes will be complete and there will no obstacles to our protection from the faults and shortcomings of saṃsāra and nirvāṇa from the side of the objects of refuge, the Three Jewels of the Mahāyāna.

With this attitude, recite the refuge prayer one hundred or one thousand times, however much you can. After this, recite the supplication prayer beginning with "Grant your blessing, so our mind may turn to the Dharma." With this supplication we pray for our practice based on the instructions from *Parting from the Four Attachments* to go well. Recite this prayer while contemplating the meaning of each of its four lines. At the end of this recitation, generate a feeling of trust that the Three Jewels see and know and that they protect you. To conclude the session, dedicate the merit gathered by going for refuge towards gaining complete enlightenment for the benefit of all sentient beings.

Please try to follow these instructions to the best of your abilities during your private meditation sessions, and in the periods between formal practice, think of the Three Jewels and recollect their qualities as often as possible.

E. On the Vows, the Training, and Observances

To take refuge in the Three Jewels, we need to obtain the refuge vows. If we have taken the bodhicitta vows or the vows of a lay follower, we already possess these vows because they are included in the preliminary part of these rituals. If we haven't received any of these vows yet, it is necessary for us to take the refuge vows. And once we have taken them, there are certain things we must observe, which I will briefly explain here.

In general, there are two areas of training for those who possess these vows: things to be adopted and things to be abandoned. Ārya Asaṅga taught the practices that followers who have taken the refuge vows should abide by as a fourfold discipline. First, once we have taken refuge in the Three Jewels, we should seek out those sublime beings who have a good understanding of the Dharma and are practitioners themselves, and take them as our teachers. Second, we should receive Dharma instructions from these individuals. Third, instead of following our own assumptions and practicing whatever and however we think, we should learn and know the conduct and practices related to our vows. We should be genuinely concerned with the training and be able to clearly distinguish the practices we ought to take up from the things we ought to abandon. And fourth, we should apply the instructions and practice as much as possible.

How to cultivate the training

I will now explain some important aspects of the training. In general, it is important to occasionally make offerings, and we should recite the refuge formula at least six times a day.

The following important points can be applied immediately. Whenever we encounter any statue or image of the Buddha, we should approach it thinking that we are meeting the actual Buddha and pay our respect by prostrating to it. It is said that merely encountering the form of a buddha accrues greater merit than that generated by worshiping an entire world filled with arhats and śrāvaka sanghas.

Similarly, when we see a stūpa containing relics of a buddha, we should view it as the wisdom mind of the Buddha and pay our respect. Since the true nature of all stūpas is the same, prostrating to any one stūpa—such as any of the three sacred stūpas of Nepal[4] for instance—is equivalent to prostrating to all the stūpas of the world. The same applies to the stūpas that are in shrine rooms. But for our encounters with these sacred images to produce such merit, we need to understand this essential point.

The Buddhist scriptures are extremely important. Why is this so? They have no mouths to teach us, but because they contain the instructions that explain to us what to do and what to abstain from, they are in fact the representatives of the Buddha's speech. We should view them in this way and treat them with great respect, keeping them in elevated places, and make offerings to them. In brief, it is said that paying homage and worshiping even a single paragraph of the Buddha's words is greatly meritorious.

In terms of the Sangha, since monastic and lay Dharma practitioners are representatives of the Sangha, we should treat them all with equal respect. Maitreya identified the actual

Sangha Jewel as the ārya bodhisattvas from the moment they attain the first bhūmi onward. It is important to note that for us, these bodhisattvas are the most sublime field of both merit and negativity, depending on how we relate to them. However, we cannot know who is and who is not a bodhisattva. We cannot say that among Dharma practitioners, only those who have formally taken the bodhicitta vow are bodhisattvas. But those who have taken these vows and have kept them intact certainly are, and we should therefore treat especially those individuals with great reverence. The Buddha stated that, generally speaking, only omniscient beings are able to know the minds and dispositions of others. Thus, ordinary beings are incapable of correctly assessing others. Why is this so? Based on their physical and verbal conduct alone, it is impossible to know the actual mental disposition of another being. The Dharma itself is faultless, but those who follow it may have many flaws. However, it is considered a great mistake to criticize and blame them for their mistakes. This is particularly true regarding monastics who we think are behaving in unworthy ways. Whenever we see a stūpa, we pay our respect because we understand what it represents, regardless of whether it contains relics or not. Similarly, the members of the monastic Sangha wear the monastic robes and possess the mark of those who follow the Awakened One. For this very reason, we should be mindful to act in respectful ways towards them.

What to avoid

Once we have taken refuge in the Buddha, we do not take gods and other teachers as our guide. Once we have taken refuge in the Dharma, we do not hurt or harm any sentient being by killing or beating them or doing any other ill. And once we have taken refuge in the Sangha, it is inappropriate to take followers of other traditions as our companions on the path.

Some scholars have added that certain sūtras explain, concerning the observance of the Dharma, that once we have taken refuge in the Dharma, we should not view practices that are not Dharma as Dharma. The most important point is never to forsake the Three Jewels, even at the cost of one's life. The Indian treatises do not explain precisely what this means. They do not indicate which actions result in the destruction of our refuge vows. Most Tibetan scholars agree that taking as one's guide anyone besides the Buddha—that is, a non-omniscient being—effectively destroys the refuge vows. However, this is not entirely clear. At any rate, we should be very careful not to forsake the Three Jewels.

F. The Benefits of Taking Refuge

We will now briefly discuss the benefits of taking refuge. By taking the refuge vows we formally become Buddhists. In other words, we become followers of the Buddha. And given that we have entered the path taught by the Buddha, the stream of suffering will one day dry up for us. It is said that the mental state of taking refuge itself is a great protection. What does this mean? It means that, at last, we are protected from the horrors of the lower realms, and in the short term, we can also be protected from many smaller forms of sufferings. Likewise, the Three Jewels and the worldly gods, nāgās, and yakṣas, who take delight in virtue and goodness, will protect us. Once we have taken refuge, we will always be connected to the Three Jewels, life after life. Many negative deeds and traits will come to an end, and we will gather great merit. It should be noted in particular that many masters have emphasized that taking refuge in the Three Jewels closes the doors to the lower realms.

The ultimate benefit obtained by taking refuge is that we will attain the level of the Triple Gem. The Kangyur contains a sūtra entitled *Taking Refuge in the Three Jewels*. In this sūtra it is recounted how one day a question about the benefits of taking refuge arose in Śāriputra's mind. With this, Śāriputra went to see the Buddha and asked, "How much merit and benefit is gathered by taking refuge?" The Buddha replied with an analogy, "If a faithful person were to build a gigantic stūpa made only of precious jewels reaching up to the level of Akaniṣṭha, that person would acquire vast merit indeed. But the merit gathered by taking refuge is far greater still."

III. ON THE THREE VEHICLES AND THE FIVE PATHS

For those who have not had the opportunity to study the great treatises in detail, the following points might be of benefit. In the teachings on the objects of refuge, we differentiated between the Sangha of the greater vehicle and the Sangha of the lesser vehicle. This might require some clarification. Nowadays, we often hear about the "three vehicles" referring to Hīnayāna, Mahāyāna, and Secret Mantrayāna. We should know, however, that most authors did not use the term in this way. Chögyal Phagpa identified these three vehicles as the uncommon classification of the three vehicles. Generally, the term *three yānas*, or "three vehicles," refers to Śrāvakayāna, Pratyekabuddhayāna, and Mahāyāna. Each of these three vehicles consists of five paths: the path of accumulation, the path of joining, the path of seeing, the path of cultivation, and the path of no further training. Thus, there are fifteen paths. The path of no further training is not a path in the true sense of the word; it refers to the result of each of the three vehicles and is merely termed a path.

The first of the five paths is called the path of accumulation. At this stage, the practitioner recognizes that both saṃsāra in general and the particular states of existence are full of flaws, and the wish to leave it behind is generated. Followers who are naturally of the Hīnayāna type will generate the thought "I must attain liberation." This is the so-called "generation of the resolve"[5] of the Hīnayāna, also referred to as the generation of the resolve to attain the smaller and middling levels of awakening. It is also called the mind of renunciation, or "definite release." To see saṃsāra as full of flaws and to then generate the thought "I must attain buddhahood to benefit sentient beings" is the generation of the resolve of the Mahāyāna, or the generation of the resolve to attain supreme awakening.

When we then receive the refuge vows, the monastic vows, or the bodhisattva vows on the basis of this resolve, we enter the various paths of awakening. This means that we enter the Mahāyāna path specifically the moment we take the bodhisattva vows on the basis of the resolve to attain buddhahood to benefit all sentient beings. The same applies to each of the three vehicles. Having generated the resolve to attain any of these three aims, we then observe the respective discipline of each path and engage mainly in the practices of hearing and reflection. This is the path of accumulation.

In this way, we gradually develop and deepen our understanding of the Dharma until we reach a stage where we develop insight mainly through meditative cultivation. This is the path of joining, the second path. Among the many meditative practices, the path of joining refers specifically to the cultivation of insight into the nonexistence of the self.

After this comes the path of seeing. At this stage, those who have entered the Hīnayāna path will have direct cognition of the nature of the four truths. Those who practice the Mahāyāna will have direct cognition of the nature of all phenomena. These two realizations are the paths of seeing for each of the two vehicles. At this moment the practitioners become āryas, or noble beings. Those on the Mahāyāna attain the first bhūmi, or bodhisattva ground. The Hīnayāna practitioners attain any of the first three levels of realization, namely those of a stream-enterer, a once-returner, or a non-returner, depending on the individual.

This is followed by the path of cultivation, where we repeatedly cultivate the direct cognition of the way things are obtained through the previous path to familiarize ourselves with this insight. The Mahāyāna path of cultivation is divided into the nine remaining bhūmis. While the path of seeing is very short—it may last for only one hour or even less—the path of cultivation takes a very long time to complete. By means of these two paths—that path of seeing and the path of cultivating—the bodhisattvas traverse the ten bhūmis of the Mahāyāna.

At the end of this process, the most powerful wisdom cognition eradicates the most subtle obscurations that can be abandoned by means of the path one has engaged in. When this is accomplished, those who have followed the Mahāyāna path attain perfect buddhahood and Hīnayāna practitioners the level of a śrāvaka arhat.

The Main Part of the Teaching on *Parting From The Four Attachments*

A Summary of the Teachings

To study these teachings, I suggest you read the Omniscient Gorampa Sönam Sengé's commentary. I will generally follow his exposition, but we will not go through his introduction.

When the Great Lama Sakyapa Kunga Nyingpo was twelve years old, he stayed in retreat for six months to practice the sādhana of Mañjughoṣa. At one point during this retreat, he had a direct vision of the protector Mañjughoṣa, who uttered the following lines:

> If you are attached to this life, you are not a Dharma practitioner.
> If you are attached to saṃsāra, you have no renunciation.
> If you are attached to your own self-interest, you have no bodhicitta.
> If there is grasping, it is not the view.

With these four lines, Mañjughoṣa summarized Pāramitāyāna practice in its entirety. He not only gave these teachings, but also taught many sūtras and instructions on this occasion. Then, Mañjughoṣa blessed Sachen Kunga Nyingpo and he obtained the ability to never forget any Dharma teaching. This was witnessed by all those present at the time. He gained not only this particular ability, but also an incomparable intelligence. The purport of these instructions is, in brief, the following:

1. "If you are attached to this life, you are not a Dharma practitioner" means that since our attachment to this life prevents us from being genuine Dharma practitioners, it is important to let go of our unskillful concerns regarding this present life.

2. "If you are attached to saṃsāra, you have no renunciation" means that to achieve liberation, we must let go of our attachment to all three realms of saṃsāra. We must give rise to the thought of renunciation, wishing to attain definite release from the whole of saṃsāra. The mind of renunciation is not the wish to merely avoid rebirth in the lower realms of existence; it includes the higher realms as well. If we are attached to even the most sublime aspects of the higher realms, we lack genuine renunciation.

3. "If you are attached to your own self-interest, you have no bodhicitta" means that since bodhisattvas are mainly working to benefit others, if we are mainly concerned with our own personal benefit, we are not bodhisattvas.

4. "If there is grasping, it is not the view." The term *view* refers to the mind that knows the true nature of things. This ultimate nature cannot be established in terms of any of the so-called extremes of conceptual elaboration. Therefore, as long as the mind is apprehending things in terms of any form of conceptual extreme, it is not the view.

In order to relinquish attachment to this life, we contemplate how difficult it is to obtain the freedoms and conducive conditions of a precious human life, death and impermanence, and the law of karma, cause and result. To let go of attachment to saṃsāra, we reflect on the faults of saṃsāra. To abandon our selfish concerns, we cultivate love, compassion, and bodhicitta. And lastly, to assimilate the meaning of the line "If there is grasping, it is not the view," we practice calm abiding and insight meditation, śamatha and vipaśyanā. For the latter it is also necessary to receive instructions on the view. This summarizes the instructions based on the mind training teaching of *Parting from the Four Attachments*.

FOUR ATTACHMENTS AND THREE LEVELS OF PRACTICE

The two most famous Mahāyāna instructions by the Indian master Jowo Jé Palden Atiśa are his teachings on *lamrim*, the stages of the path, and on *lojong*, or mind training. The former are his common instructions, and the latter are the instructions he transmitted to his most advanced disciples.

The teachings on the stages of the path are divided into three levels of practice in accordance with the three types of followers of inferior, middling, and superior scope. Individuals of inferior scope aim at not being reborn in the lower realms in their next and future lives and at obtaining higher rebirths. Those with the goal of attaining liberation for themselves are identified as individuals of middling scope, and those of superior scope wish to attain buddhahood for the benefit of others. To suit the dispositions with these three types of practitioners, Atiśa taught three types of Dharma. The Dharma for individuals of inferior scope is the practice of wholesome deeds to ensure a good rebirth. The Dharma for individuals of middling scope is the practice of the three higher trainings leading to liberation. The Dharma for individuals of superior scope is the Mahāyāna path of bodhicitta, the six perfections, and so forth.

As the Dharma path can be classified into these three basic categories, we must make sure that our practice is at the very least motivated by the wish to benefit our future life. This level of practice is indicated with the words "If you are attached to this life, you are not a Dharma practitioner." It corresponds to the path in common with individuals of inferior scope. The line "If you are attached to saṃsāra, you have no renunciation" reflects the path in common with individuals of middling scope.

The last two lines of the instructions on *Parting from the Four Attachments* indicate the uncommon path for individuals of superior scope. This Mahāyāna path has two components: method and wisdom. The line "If you are attached to your own self-interest, you have no bodhicitta" indicates the method aspect, and "If there is grasping, it is not the view" the wisdom aspect. Any practice we perform free from these four attachments, even a single repetition of taking refuge, becomes a Mahāyāna practice and thus the path to buddhahood.

A Commentary on the Supplication Prayer

Our daily recitations include a supplication prayer that is recited after taking refuge. Since it is related to the four lines of *Parting from the Four Attachments*, I will explain its meaning here. The second line of this supplication relates to the first instruction and reads,

> "Grant your blessing, so that our minds may turn towards the Dharma."

By parting from attachment to this life, our minds turn towards the Dharma and we will be able engage in genuine Dharma practice. The next line reads,

> "Grant your blessing, so that we may take the Dharma as our path."

By parting from attachment to the whole of saṃsāra, that is, when the mind is truly free of any attachment to the three realms of existence, every practice we perform will become a path leading to liberation. Conversely, when we observe our discipline because of the wish to gain a good rebirth, for instance, this practice will become a cause for saṃsāra and not a liberating path.

> "Grant your blessing, so that mistakes on the path may be allayed."

There are two major mistakes on the Mahāyāna which are related to the method and wisdom aspects of the path respectively: to be attached to one's personal benefit and to have any form of conceptual grasping with regard to ultimate reality. This supplication thus relates to the last two lines of the instructions of Mañjughoṣa.

The First Line:
"If You Are Attached to This Life, You Are Not a Dharma Practitioner."

Introduction

We will now discuss each of the four lines in some detail. The first instruction reads, "If you are attached to this life, you are not a Dharma practitioner." However, just telling ourselves "Don't be attached to this life!" will not work. Our mind will not listen. Why? Because it is not independent. Our mind is presently dominated by mental afflictions. This is why we need a method to let go of our attachment to this life. This method consists of contemplating the difficult-to-obtain freedoms and positive conditions of a precious human life, death and impermanence, and the law of karma, deeds and their results. Of this, the actual antidote to overcome our attachment to this life—and therefore the main practice—is the recollection of death and impermanence. The contemplation of precious human birth functions as the best preparation for it, and reflection on the law of karma as an auxiliary practice.

Our attachment to this life translates into attachment to what is called the *eight worldly dharmas*. It refers to eight things that ordinary human beings are constantly concerned with: happiness and suffering, gain and loss of wealth, praise and blame, and renown and ill repute. We enjoy and desire happiness, gain, praise, and renown, while we dislike their opposites: suffering, loss, blame, and ill repute. This is what is referred to as attachment to the eight worldly concerns, in other words, attachment to this life.

Why is it so important that we overcome these attachments? This life lasts just a moment; it is so very fleeting. Being attached to these eight concerns is therefore not only useless, but it becomes a real problem. In the Lamdré teachings, it is explained that our attachment to this life is in fact the main obstacle to genuine and pure Dharma practice. Because of this attachment, we initially lack interest in the Dharma and don't even enter the path. And even if we do practice a bit, our practice will be riddled with flaws; it will not be genuine Dharma practice. It is like adding poison to otherwise nutritious food: if the Dharma we practice is contaminated with these eight dharmas, it becomes ineffective and even harmful. Regardless of what we do—whether we maintain our ethical discipline; study, reflect, and meditate; expound or listen to the teachings; or build monasteries, institutes of Buddhist learning, and stūpas—if we are motivated by these eight worldly concerns, it will only benefit this life. Beyond that, they may even become causes for rebirth in the lower realm. Even though such Dharma activities may appear beneficial, they have no real benefit.

When it says that we should give up our attachment to this life, it does not mean that we must give up all our money and possessions to live a life of hardships. This approach to the path through austerity is opposed to the Buddhist tradition. Our teacher the Buddha himself endured intense austerity when he devoted himself to the path of ascetic practice for six years. However, he never declared this to be the path to liberation. On the contrary, having realized that this approach does not yield the desired results, he abandoned this path, accepted appropriate food and clothing, restored his health, and went to Bodhgaya to meditate. Then, in just one single night, he attained perfect awakening. In this way, he showed by example to those on mistaken paths that, while the practice of proper forms of meditation is indeed very important, such ascetic practice does not lead to accomplishment.

The two main activities related to the Dharma are study and practice. Students require conducive conditions, like proper food, textbooks, and so forth. All of these need to be provided, as the lack of important resources makes a great difference. Meditators in particular need conducive conditions, such as nutritious and healthy food, to support their practice. From the recipient's side, it is a serious fault to accept such resources provided by devoted benefactors, and then to neglect one's studies or the practice. However, students and meditators have to accept support when it is offered to them. Therefore, if they accept just the amount of donations they actually need with the thought that it shall be beneficial for the others and subsequently engage in study and practice, they do not incur the fault of wasting offerings made by the faithful. In a sūtra it is stated that, while building a stūpa the size of the entire world generates vast merit, even greater merit is accrued by providing the conditions for one single person to study the Dharma. Supporting just one meditator, then, produces even more merit than supporting many thousands of Dharma students.

I. THE FREEDOMS AND CONDUCIVE CONDITIONS SO DIFFICULT TO OBTAIN

When we meditate on precious human life with its difficult-to-obtain freedoms and conducive conditions, we first sit down on a comfortable seat and take refuge. Following the earlier instructions on taking refuge, we take refuge as much as possible. If we practice in accordance with the Sūtra tradition, we do not need to take refuge in the guru as a separate object of refuge. If we do want to recite the line "We take refuge in the guru," we should add it after taking refuge in the Sangha. If we practice in accordance with the Mantra tradition, we recite the text as it is written, beginning with taking refuge in the guru.

After the refuge practice, we recite the four lines of supplication, beginning with "Grant your blessing, so our minds may turn towards the Dharma." This is followed by the generation of bodhicitta: "In order to benefit all sentient beings, I must attain buddhahood. For this purpose, I am meditating on the instructions of *Parting from the Four Attachments*."

For the main practice on the difficult-to-obtain freedoms and conducive conditions, we begin by thinking in general terms about the physical support necessary to practice the Dharma. Among the six types of beings wandering in saṃsāra, the human body is said to be ideal for this purpose. Then, we contemplate how difficult it is to obtain such a body endowed with all the conditions needed to cultivate the path. Once obtained, we can accomplish so many things. To have such a support is therefore of great significance and has enormous benefits. Since we possess it now, we must not waste it but use it well by practicing the Dharma.

There are four approaches to contemplate how difficult it is to obtain the freedoms and conducive conditions of a precious human life: in terms of its nature, in terms of its causes, in terms of the odds, and by means of analogy.

A. The Nature of a Precious Human Life

To reflect on the precious human life in terms of its nature, we reflect on what are called the eight freedoms and the ten riches. *Freedoms* means that we are free to practice the Dharma, that we are not constrained by certain conditions that would make this impossible. We have to realize that the life we presently have is free of the eight specific conditions that are definite obstacles to the path. In other words, we are very fortunate not to be born into any of these eight states and now to have the opportunity to practice the Dharma. *Riches* refers to the conditions that are supporting our Dharma practice. Of these, five are conditions that we ourselves must fulfill and five correspond to outer conditions. In this way, there are a total of eighteen conditions—eight freedoms and ten riches—that are needed to follow the path of Dharma. Since it is so difficult to obtain a human birth endowed with all eighteen conditions, such a life is called a precious human life. To learn about the details of these eighteen conditions, we can refer to various textbooks and then contemplate the subject in this way.[1]

B. The Causes for a Precious Human Life

Next, we contemplate how difficult it is to obtain such a precious human life by reflecting on its causes. All the things we see around us require certain causes and conditions to come into being. The same goes for the human body. Its cause is powerful wholesome karma, such as the observance of ethical discipline like the monastic code. Since it is very rare for individuals to keep these vows, the result—the obtainment of a human body endowed with the eight freedoms and the ten riches—is rare as well. Most sentient beings engage in many negative deeds. As a result of these actions they are born, life after life, in the lower realms. It is very rare indeed for them to obtain a human life. We should contemplate along these lines over and over again.

C. The Odds of Obtaining a Precious Human Life

After this, we contemplate the precious human life from the perspective of the odds of obtaining such a birth. Among the six types of beings, most go from the higher realms to the lower realms of existence. Therefore, very few ever obtain a human life.

Presently, we can see only two types of beings: humans and animals. Even here, the numbers are incomparable. If we go to a stream or a spring in the summertime, we can see that the number of creatures living in the water can exceed the entire human population. Or consider the number of insects and other organisms living in and around a single tree in the forest. They are countless. This is how we can contemplate the precious human life from the perspective of the odds of obtaining it, compared to all other forms of life. We should repeat those and similar thoughts until we come to truly appreciate this fact.

D. Analogies

When a handful of peas is thrown at a wall, it is very unlikely that any of the peas will stick on that wall. Similarly, the likelihood of sentient beings obtaining a human life is very slim.

Another analogy illustrates the difficulty of obtaining a precious human life as follows: Imagine a single wooden yoke floating in the great ocean, tossed around by the winds coming from all directions. In that ocean lives a blind turtle that surfaces only once every hundred years. Given these conditions, it is almost impossible for the head of that turtle to pass through the yoke. It is said that obtaining the support of a human body is just as difficult.

If, now that we have obtained it, we use it wisely in accordance with the Dharma, we will be able to accomplish not merely the wishes of this life, but higher rebirths in our future lives, as well as liberation and even buddhahood. This human body is therefore of immeasurable value. No other possession, no matter how precious, can help us carry out this work and accomplish such important aims. It is important that we recognize this to appreciate the great benefit and purpose this life can fulfill.

For example, someone who tries to go to the United States and was able to acquire an airplane ticket with great difficulty will certainly not oversleep the day of their departure and miss their flight. Our human life is like that plane: we need its support to cross the ocean of saṃsāra. If we want to attain liberation we have to practice the Dharma, and for this we require this human life.

II. Death and Impermanence

The subject of death and impermanence is very important for our practice. We might be convinced of the importance of Dharma practice, but most of us might think that it is alright to put it off to later. This is laziness. We therefore require a skillful means to stop such thoughts of procrastination. This is precisely the function of the contemplation on death and impermanence. We should therefore reflect and meditate on this subject from today onward. It will help us tremendously in our Dharma practice.

This subject has three divisions: reflecting on the certainty of death, reflecting on the uncertainty of the time of death, and reflecting on the fact that nothing except for the Dharma will help us when the time does come. For each of these points, we use three reasonings to guide our contemplation.

A. Death is Certain

This contemplation is based on three reasonings to establish the certainty of death in us.

First, our birth is the very reason why we will certainly die.

Second, our bodies are very fragile and can easily perish, like a bubble on water. When this body is burned, nothing will remain of it but a pile of ashes. There is nothing lasting about it.

Third, our lifespan continuously decreases. From the very beginning of this life and with every passing minute, hour, day, month, and year, the time we have left keeps becoming less and less. There is no way to increase our lifespan once it is exhausted; we are not able to add some extra time to it.

B. The Time of Death is Uncertain

This contemplation is of particular importance. Here, too, we have three reasonings to guide the reflection.

First, as human beings born into the world of Jambudvīpa, we do not have a definite lifespan. If we did, we could predict the time of our death, but this is impossible for us. This is the first reason why the time of our death is uncertain.

The other two reasons we contemplate here are the fact that the conditions that keep us alive are very few, while countless conditions can cause our death. Indeed, there is nothing we could clearly identify as something that could never be a condition for our demise. Even the things that sustain our life, like food and medicine, can bring about our death. When the time of certain death has come, nothing can avert it. Until this time comes, we can use many methods to cheat death, by seeking medical treatment, receiving long-life empowerments, accomplishing long-life practices, and so forth. But when the time has come, even the perfectly awakened buddhas are unable to prevent our death.

C. Nothing Except for the Dharma Will Be of Help

At the time of death, our relatives, friends, or whoever might be with us will not be able to help us. Why is that so? The suffering of dying cannot be shared with others, and when we die, we will leave alone. Not one person with us now will come with us.

Our possessions will be of no benefit whatsoever. Why? Because we will go alone, naked and empty-handed.

Our name and social standing will provide no help at all. Some scholars mention as a third point that one's body is of no benefit at the time of death—rather than one's status—because it will be left behind at that point.

At any rate, during our life we engage in many negative deeds, be it for the sake of those close and dear to us, for the pleasure and well-being of the body, to acquire food and clothing, to gain social recognition, or to avoid losing what we have. It is a matter of fact that all of these things will be left behind, but we will carry with us the weight of the negative actions carried out for their sake. This is why it is so important to contemplate along these lines and accustom ourselves with these thoughts. If we do so over and over again, we will begin to be acutely aware of the reality of death. With this mindset, we will have no time for any activities other than the practice of Dharma.

We can compare the activities we carry out for the benefit of this life with building a house for the sole purpose of resting in it for a short while. How long do we need to rest? Maybe just a few hours or a few days at most. It would be senseless to spend so much time building a house for this purpose alone, wouldn't it?

From now on, whenever we plan to carry out any activities, we should call an internal meeting. The awareness of death and impermanence should be invited as one of the main members in these meetings and we should listen to its opinion. This will make a big difference in our decision-making process.

In his commentary, Gorampa states: "This is the main method to bring the mind to the Dharma." This means that the thought of death is the most effective method to make our Dharma practice genuine and pure. We should therefore always keep in mind the impermanence of this life when we engage in our daily activities outside formal meditation sessions. When we eat, we should consider, "At the moment I have this good food, but one day I won't be able to swallow even a single bite. This time will certainly come." When we put on clothes, we should think, "I dress up in these fine clothes, but soon only one set of clothes will be needed to dress this body, then a corpse." When we are with family and friends, engaged in conversation, we should internally remember, "I may be in good company now, but soon we will all part ways." These and many similar reflections are taught in the sūtras. We should keep them in mind and recollect death and impermanence repeatedly.

Gyalsé Tokmé stated:

> When a continued awareness of death and impermanence has been born, it won't be difficult for us to practice the Dharma. When genuine compassion has arisen, it won't be difficult for us to work for others' well-being and benefit. When we have grown accustomed to the understanding of no-self, it won't be difficult for us to abandon the afflictions.

When our teacher Buddha Śākyamuni displayed his passing into parinirvāṇa, he said: "All compounded phenomena are impermanent." These are said to be his final words.

We can lead a very good and successful life simply by acting in accordance with the Dharma and by avoiding inflicting harm on others. This can be accomplished even without the support of the Dharma. At the time of death, however, nothing except for the Dharma will be of benefit to us. This underlines the importance of the Dharma: it is indispensable at that time. This is illustrated by means of numerous analogies in the sūtras. When we are sick, we need medicine; when poor, we are in need of resources; to travel we require money, cars, and planes; when hungry we need food, and when thirsty, drink. In the same way, we absolutely need the Dharma when the hour of death has arrived.

III. Karma: Actions and Their Results

We can all see that there are vast differences between the various countries and regions of the world: some environments are very pleasant for us and others are extremely harsh. Similarly, there are many different species and types of sentient beings inhabiting the earth, and all differ in terms of the happiness and suffering they experience. Where do these differences come from? Some religious or secular traditions maintain that these occur randomly, without any cause as such. Others believe that this is the doing of a supreme being. In accordance with the Buddha's teaching, we believe that all of this is the display of dependent arising, brought about through the interaction of specific causes and conditions. Furthermore, the outer environment we share arises on the basis of common karma, and the bodies of sentient beings stem from the particular karma unique to each individual. Generally, three types of karma are distinguished—unwholesome, wholesome, and neutral—and we will discuss each in turn.

A. Unwholesome Karma

When we contemplate the law of karma in terms of unwholesome karma, we must first understand its nature, then know what kind of actions bring about what kind of results, and finally repeatedly cultivate the resolve to abandon all kinds of unwholesome deeds.

First, what makes an action unwholesome? It depends on the motivation. Any karma motivated by the mental afflictions of desire, hatred or ignorance is unwholesome. The word *karma* simply means action.

Desire, as one of the roots of unwholesome deeds, means relishing and being attached to the things and entities of worldly existence which are perceived as the causes and conditions for well-being and happiness.

Hatred means aversion and mental unrest focused on objects perceived as sources of suffering and dissatisfaction.

Ignorance, in this context, means the mental factor that is confused about which actions of body, speech, and mind are to be adopted and which to be abandoned to achieve happiness and avoid suffering.

1. The ten unwholesome deeds

There are so many different kinds of unwholesome deeds, but they can be condensed into the ten most important unwholesome actions: three pertain to acts of the body, four to speech, and three to the mind.

Killing

The first of the three unwholesome physical actions is killing. It means to intentionally and unerringly end the life of another sentient being. To kill *intentionally* means that if we inadvertently step on an insect and kill it, we do not incur the karmic fault of killing. *Unerringly* means that if someone plans to kill an enemy, for example, but accidently kills another instead, they do not incur the fault of the main act of killing. The phrase *another sentient being* implies that when someone commits suicide, they too do not incur the fault of the main act of killing. The full act of killing occurs when someone harms another being with the intention of killing and that individual then dies as a result of one's action. The fault of killing also occurs if one orders someone else to kill another.

Taking what is not given

Taking what is not given means stealing and robbing. It applies to kings or rulers who appropriate others' belongings to deprive them of their property by force, just as it does to common thieves who deceive their victims and remain unnoticed in their crime. The aspects of intentionality and of acting in an unerring manner must be present here as well to qualify as a complete act of stealing. The act is also committed if one orders or entices another to steal.

Sexual misconduct

Sexual misconduct can occur in four ways: (1) with an inappropriate partner, that is, the partner of another with whom it is not appropriate to have sexual relations; (2) at an inappropriate place, that is, a place with the representation of enlightened body, speech, and mind; (3) at an inappropriate time, that is, during the day or when one's wife or partner is pregnant, as well as when one has taken the one-day precepts of a lay practitioner; and (4) through an inappropriate passage, that is, oral or anal intercourse.

Here, too, the action must be carried out without mistake or else the fault of the complete act of sexual misconduct does not occur. This means that sexual activity as such does not constitute sexual misconduct. Furthermore, if one orders someone else to engage in an inappropriate sexual activity, it is not a complete act of sexual misconduct on one's own part.

If it is motivated by any of the three root afflictions, a sexual deed—like any other action—becomes an unwholesome action. This can be illustrated with the act of killing. When someone kills an animal out of desire to eat its meat or to sell it to make money, it is killing motivated by desire. When one kills an enemy, it is killing motivated by hatred. When one kills to make a red offering or blood sacrifice, thinking it will bring some benefit, it is killing motivated by ignorance. The other unwholesome actions can be classified in the same way based on the motivation underlying the deed.

Lying

Of the four unwholesome verbal actions, the first is lying. The act of lying is complete when one speaks falsehood to someone with the intention of lying, and that person has understood what was said.

Divisive speech

When one speaks with the intention to divide two parties—regardless of whether they are in harmony or not, and regardless of whether one speaks the truth or not—and they have understood what was said, the unwholesome act of divisive speech has been committed.

Hurtful speech

The fault of hurtful speech occurs when one verbally abuses or slanders another and they have heard it.

Idle talk

Idle talk is a vast topic. It can be singing songs, if our singing is motivated by mental afflictions. It can be flattering a sponsor or supporter, or speaking of war, of prostitution, and so forth. Furthermore, if, inspired by faith, we recite the scriptures of other religions, this too is considered idle talk. Here, it does not depend on whether others hear what we say. Simply using our speech in such ways constitutes the unwholesome deed of idle talk. And if we order others to engage in any of these four acts of speech, we incur the respective fault ourselves.

As mentioned earlier, for these seven actions of body and speech to be unwholesome, they must be motivated by mental afflictions. If such motivation is not present, these deeds, including the act of killing, are not necessarily unwholesome actions. They can be wholesome or neutral as well depending on the motivation.

Covetousness

Covetousness is the first of the three mental unwholesome actions. It is the wish that the possession or whatever one finds pleasant and appealing belonging to another comes to oneself instead.

Ill-will

Ill-will is the thought and intention to harm another.

Wrong views

Wrong views means to think that there is no law of karma, and no past and future lives, and to believe that there are no Three Jewels. If we are merely unsure about these things, it is doubt—not a wrong view. To constitute a wrong view, we must be convinced that there is in fact no karma and so forth.

The seven unwholesome deeds of body and speech are listed in an order of decreasing severity, with the first being the most negative deed and the last the least severe. With the three mental unwholesome deeds it is the opposite; the first is less severe than the second, which is less negative than the third.

2. *Their results*

An action will produce several types of result. The so-called "result of full maturation" of the ten unwholesome deeds is rebirth in the three lower realms of existence. Each of these deeds can be of lesser, middling, or greater strength. This depends on various factors such as recurrence, intensity of motivation, and one's own perception of the action. If a given negative deed has been committed many times, with a strong motivation, without remorse, without thinking that it was wrong to act in this way, and, on top of lacking shame and embarrassment during the act, if one was experiencing a sense of gladness and was thinking that it was good to commit it, then it becomes a powerful unwholesome action. If these factors are of middling intensity, the act is of middling strength, and if they are weak, it is a lesser unwholesome deed.

The result of full maturation of a powerful negative action is rebirth in the hell realm, that of a middling negative action is rebirth as a hungry ghost, and that of a lesser unwholesome deed is rebirth as an animal.

In terms of the motivation, unwholesome actions driven by hatred project rebirth into the hell realm, those motivated by desire to a hungry ghost existence, and those prompted by ignorance to a rebirth in the animal kingdom. For example, if someone is in a state of intense anger, a single negative word spoken can be a complete cause for a birth in the hell realm.

Another type of result is called "result similar to the cause." This has two aspects: an experience similar to the cause and deeds similar to the cause. The experience similar to the cause can be as follows: After having been born in the lower realms as a result of a complete act of killing, one may obtain a human birth which will be of short duration as a result of the same action. This is the experience similar to the cause. The corresponding result of stealing is the experience of poverty, and that of sexual misconduct is the inability to find a good life partner. Deeds similar to the cause means that, as a result of having killed in the past, one wishes to do it again and even finds joy in it. Some people have a natural liking for stealing for example. These are deeds similar to the cause.

A third type of result is called the "dominant result." This result ripens as the outer environment. For example, the dominant result of the act of killing is to be born in an unappealing environment where one will not have a dwelling. The dominant result of stealing is to be born in a place that has either an excess or a lack of rain. The dominant result of sexual misconduct is birth in a polluted or impoverished environment and the inability to leave such a place. An arid or infertile land means that it will be difficult to cultivate good crops, which in turn means that the food consumed there is not nutritious. This leads to poor health and being prone to disease. Furthermore, such regions are more likely to experience many conflicts and wars. One may also be born in places infested with dangerous wildlife or with thieves, robbers, and bandits. All of these are the dominant result of unwholesome deeds.

In brief, all suffering and everything unwanted is the result of unwholesome actions. In the end, their function is to harm oneself. Realizing that we have committed many such actions in the past and that it was wrong to act in these ways, we feel remorse for our misdeeds. Based on this, we firmly resolve never to repeat our past mistakes and to completely abstain from such negative deeds from now on, even if our life depends on it. In this way, we can purify our past misdeeds and prevent ourselves from repeating them in the future. This is why it is so important to confess our negative deeds in this way.

3. How to confess negative deeds by means of the four powers

There are many ways to confess our negative actions. It is said that the most important point in confession is to employ all four powers. These are the power of remorse, the power of support, the power of remedial action, and the power of resolve.

The power of remorse means to feel sincere remorse for our past negative deeds, just as we would regret having ingested poison when we understand the harm it produces.

The power of support means that we rely on an object that is able to protect us from negativity and harm, just as we would rely on medicine.

Concerning the power of remedial action, six practices are mentioned in particular: reading the sūtras, meditating on emptiness, reciting mantras such as the hundred-syllable mantra, manufacturing buddha statues, making offerings to the buddhas and their representations, and memorizing and repeating the names of the buddhas and bodhisattvas.

The power of resolve is the firm determination that, having purified our misdeeds through confession, we will not engage in them ever again.

Furthermore, it is important to purify our negative deeds as quickly as possible. As soon as we realize our mistake, we can confess by reciting verses like this one, taken from a Seven-Limb liturgy:

> I take refuge in the Three Jewels,
> And confess each and every one of my negative deeds.

B. Wholesome Karma and its Results

Fundamentally, there are three roots of wholesome deeds, which are the mind free of desire, free of hatred, and free of ignorance. With this, any actions of the body, speech, or mind motivated by faith, love, compassion, and so forth are referred to as wholesome deeds.

Furthermore, when we abstain from the ten unwholesome actions and then either take the vows of a lay practitioner based on such a motivation or simply promise and resolve never to commit such actions again, this is called engaging in the ten wholesome actions.

The results of wholesome deeds are the opposite of the results of unwholesome actions explained earlier. For instance, the result of full maturation of wholesome deeds is rebirth in the higher realms to obtain the body of a god or a human. The experience similar to the cause resulting from abstaining from killing is to have a long life and so forth. The action similar to the cause is that one naturally enjoys accomplishing wholesome deeds. The dominant result is to be born in a good environment, to have a good livelihood, good food, good clothes, and so on.

Moreover, if one has relinquished all ten negative deeds with the motivation to awaken in accordance with the teachings of the Hīnayāna, one will attain the level of an arhat as a result of one's course of action. If one has done so with the bodhicitta motivation of the Mahāyāna, one will accomplish buddhahood.

C. What Determines the Strength of Our Actions?

The strength of our deeds, both wholesome and unwholesome, can vary greatly, depending on various factors. For instance, if a practitioner has been in the habit of circumambulating a stūpa every single day, a single circumambulation of theirs will be much more powerful than a single circumambulation made by someone who has not been practicing in this way. The efficacy of an action will be also determined by the intensity of the motivation and whether one acted out of one's own accord or not. It will also depend on the presence or absence of an antidote. For instance, if one regrets an action, it will become less powerful. This applies to both negative and positive deeds. If one is honest about one's misdeeds and confesses them openly to others, their faults will be purified. Conversely, boasting about one's good deeds in front of others will reduce the strength of their potential.

Furthermore, the strength of the action is also determined by the objects we relate to. For example, if the object is the Three Jewels, making an offering out of sincere devotion will be a powerful wholesome action, and showing disrespect will be a similarly powerful unwholesome deed. Likewise, taking care of one's parents is a powerful good deed, and harming them a serious misdeed. Also, the potential of any action is enhanced if it is performed in the presence of a representation of the Three Jewels, as well as when it is carried out on special occasions. It is said that the power of our actions is multiplied by seven million on the four holy days commemorating the Buddha's activities.

D. When Does Karma Ripen?

It is furthermore very important for us to understand when the results of our actions will be experienced. In this context, two types of karmic results are distinguished: the results that are certain to be experienced and those that are not. The results of very powerful karma will be experienced without doubt. Deeds performed with a distracted mind, however, such as reciting prayers while thinking of something else, will not produce results that are certain to be experienced.

There are three types of karma whose results will surely be experienced. The first type, as mentioned above, is powerful actions, such as benefiting or harming one's parents. Such deeds can produce their result in this very life, which is why they are called "karma experienced in the visible world." Some of our actions will bear their karmic fruit in the next life. These are called "karma experienced after birth." The third type of action will ripen in any life after the next one. These are referred to as "karma experienced at other times." Even karma that will not produce its result for a long time won't lose its efficacy. It will ripen when its time has come. It is important that we understand the laws of karma to know how actions produce their results. The master Müchen Sempa Chenpo wrote a wonderful exposition on karma in his commentary on mind training.[2] We should be sure to study it.

E. Neutral Karma

Neutral karma are actions that are motivated neither by mental afflictions nor by a wholesome mind, such as sleep, eating food, putting on clothes, and so forth. It is not absolutely necessary to explain these types of actions. In fact, Künkhyen Gorampa does not mention them in his commentary, because they do not produce any kind of pleasant or unpleasant results. However, it is possible to transform neutral deeds into wholesome actions with the right means, as briefly explained earlier.[3] For example, when taking a seat, we can think, "May all beings attain the vajra seat of awakening;" when we go outside, "May all get out of saṃsāra;" when going to bed, "May all attain the dharmakāya," and so forth.

In brief, if we make vast aspirations towards the benefit of all beings when we engage in neutral activities, these deeds will be transformed into wholesome actions. If we are able to apply this method skillfully, we can gather vast merit every single day without much effort. This is why it is highly advised to practice in this way.

IV. DHARMA AND ONE'S ATTACHMENT TO THIS LIFE

By familiarizing ourselves with the three methods described up to this point[4] and cultivating them repeatedly, we will eventually be able to cut through our attachment to this life and stop being preoccupied with it. Then, we will no longer engage in activities that go against the Dharma. If we can practice in this way, we will become genuinely great Dharma practitioners. This represents the path of a practitioner of the highest caliber.

If we are not able to reach that level yet, we should at the very least be mindful not to engage in our Dharma activities out of attachment to this life. If we study or reflect on the Dharma with nothing but worldly benefits in mind, this Dharma will not benefit us after this life.

There is a story about Jowo Jé Palden Atiśa and one of his disciples that illustrates this point. One day, the disciple asked his master, "Should I engage in intensive meditation practice?" to which Atiśa replied, "That won't be good. Don't go meditating." "Well then, should I teach the Dharma?" the disciple asked, but the master simply repeated, "That wouldn't be good either." Finally, the student asked, "Please tell me, what should I do?" "Stop being concerned with this life!"

Someone then asked, "What happens when one engages in Dharma activities for the purpose of this life?" "Such actions will bear fruit in this life." "What will happen in the next life?" "One might be reborn in hell or in the realm of hungry ghosts."

Indeed, if we carry out Dharma activities motivated by some benefit in this life, our actions are not actually Dharma. If we practice in order to avoid rebirth in the lower realms or to obtain a higher rebirth, our Dharma will still be a cause for rebirth in saṃsāra, and thus not a genuine path leading to liberation from mental afflictions and suffering. If we practice with the intention of obtaining our individual liberation, any Dharma we engage in becomes the Hīnayāna path. It is therefore very important that we have the intention to attain buddhahood so that we can best benefit all sentient beings. With this motivation, any Dharma practice we do will be free of the three attachments: to this life, to saṃsāra, and to our personal benefit.

When we study or teach the Dharma, we should always begin with the generation of bodhicitta and conclude with the practice of dedication. In fact, any wholesome deeds we might accomplish should be blessed by the thought of bodhicitta in the beginning. The main action itself should be carried out free of conceptual fixation. This means that we should maintain an awareness of the lack of inherent existence, knowing that the root of goodness we are generating is not truly existent. After the action is completed, we should dedicate its merit.

Belief in the law of karma is the right worldly view. It is so important that people develop this view, since a conviction in the process of actions and their results will help them avoid rebirth in the lower realms.

V. DRAKPA GYALTSEN'S PITH INSTRUCTIONS

In his verses on *Parting from the Four Attachments*, Jetsün Rinpoche Drakpa Gyaltsen states in relation to the attachment to this life:

> First, relinquish attachment to this life:
> If you engage in discipline, hearing, contemplation, and meditation
> Focused on this life, you are not a Dharma practitioner.
> Give up such practice!

If we accomplish wholesome deeds, such as guarding our discipline and so forth, to achieve benefits in this life, we are not actually engaged in Dharma practice. It is best to stop this kind of practice.

> To begin with, discipline is explained as
> The root that accomplishes the higher realms,
> The stairway that leads to liberation,
> And the antidote that relinquishes suffering.

This means that discipline is necessary to obtain a body of the higher realms, to gain liberation, and to overcome the sufferings of the lower realms and of saṃsāra in general. In other words, one requires discipline in order not to be reborn in saṃsāra. Therefore, Drakpa Gyaltsen says:

> Thus, discipline is indispensable.

Since discipline is a must to achieve any of these aims, it is essential that we observe the vows and precepts we have taken.

However, if our discipline is based on attachment to this life, it will lead to all kinds of flaws in our practice. This is explained in the next verses:

> Discipline based on attachment to this life, however,
> Is the root that accomplishes the eight worldly concerns,
> It generates contempt for those with bad discipline,
> And jealousy towards those who observe it well.

With this kind of attitude, our discipline will accomplish nothing but worldly concerns, that is, our desire for praise and renown, for prosperity and so forth. Moreover, we will despise those who are unable to keep their vows purely or who conduct themselves in ways we deem incorrect. We will be jealous of those who maintain their discipline better than we do and will find ourselves criticizing them.

> It turns one's discipline into a facade
> And sows the seeds of the lower realms.
> Give up such fake discipline!

We must really take care that our own discipline does not become mere hypocrisy. If we observe pure conduct out of pretense, to give a certain impression, it is hypocrisy. What kind of results will such discipline produce? It will lead us to the lower realms. Therefore, we better drop such false discipline at once.

We might then wonder, "But isn't it necessary to observe a certain discipline?" It is indeed! What we must do is change the motivation with which we observe our discipline and the vows we have taken. If we can correct and improve our motivation, then our discipline is the foundation for the attainment of the higher realms, for liberation, and to relinquish all suffering. It is this kind of excellent discipline we should adopt and cultivate.

Then, Drakpa Gyaltsen continues:

> Those who pursue hearing and reflection
> Possess the wealth to acquire all objects of knowledge,
> The torch that dispels ignorance,
> Familiarity with the path to guide wanderers,
> And the seed of the dharmakāya.

To *acquire all objects of knowledge* means to be well-educated and learned. It indicates that the function of hearing and reflection is to enrich our education, providing us with the wealth of the various fields of knowledge. Another function of hearing and reflection is to dispel our twofold ignorance: not knowing which actions to adopt and which to abandon, and not knowing the true nature of phenomena. Also, with the knowledge thus acquired, one will one day be able not only to accomplish one's own aims, but also to guide others on the path to liberation. Finally, since hearing and reflection constitute the accumulation of wisdom, they plant the seed of the attainment of the dharmakāya. For these reasons, Drakpa Gyaltsen says:

> Hearing and reflection are indispensable.

This means that unless we engage in hearing and reflection, there is absolutely no way for us to achieve any of these aims. Why? Because, to properly engage in the path, we need to know and understand the Dharma we are practicing, and to achieve that, we must study the Buddha's teaching. Conversely, if we do not study the Dharma, we won't understand well what we are doing and we won't be able to practice correctly. But we must beware:

> Hearing and reflection based on attachment to this life, however,
> Produces a wealth of arrogance,
> Contempt for those of lesser hearing and reflection,
> And jealousy towards those well-accomplished in hearing and reflection.

With these words, Drakpa Gyaltsen directly addresses those among us engaged in the study of texts, heeding us to check whether we are motivated by attachment to this life. If we can detect within ourselves any of the signs or flaws mentioned above, it is a clear indication that our hearing and reflection is motivated by this attachment. If we study and reflect on the Dharma with worldly intentions, we will become very arrogant once disciples start to follow us and when we acquire wealth through our activities. We look down on those who have studied less than us, as well as those who have not studied at all, and feel jealous of those who are superior in this regard.

> One will seek out followers and wealth,
> And possess the root to accomplish the lower realms.
> Give up hearing and reflection based on the eight worldly concerns!

Furthermore, we will try to gain followers and wealth by teaching the Dharma. This kind of hearing and reflection is the root to accomplish the lower realms, that is, it will be the cause for an awful rebirth in the future. It would therefore be best to drop this kind of hearing and reflection motivated by the eight worldly concerns.

> Those who train in meditation
> Possess the remedy to eliminate the afflictions,
> The root to accomplish the path of liberation,
> The wealth to realize the true nature,
> And the seed of buddhahood.

Since the afflictions present in our mindstream cannot be eliminated by means of hearing and reflection alone, we really must train in meditation. This is crucial. The causes of saṃsāra are defiled karma and afflictions. Without proficiency in meditation, it is not possible to free ourselves from their results, which are the six realms of saṃsāra. However, if we do train in meditation, we will eventually be able to overcome the afflictions and thus attain the level of an arhat. Based on the training in meditation, we will also gain the wealth of discriminating wisdom that clearly cognizes the true nature of all phenomena. Ultimately, meditation will allow us to attain the level of perfect awakening or buddhahood to benefit others. This is meant by *the seed of buddhahood*. Therefore,

> Meditation is indispensable.

Since we will neither attain buddhahood nor accomplish any of these temporary aims without training in meditation, we must be sure to engage in it.

> But those who meditate, yet are focused on this life,
> Are busy even in seclusion,

> Turn their recitations into meaningless chatter,
> Disparage those who are engaged in hearing and reflection,
> And are jealous of other meditators.

These are some of the many signs that indicate that our practice is rooted in attachment to this life. To engage in sustained meditation practice, it is important to stay alone, in seclusion, away from populated and busy environments. Meditators who are motivated by the eight worldly concerns might first retreat to a lofty mountain cabin, but then invite others, only to remain busy entertaining their guests. The term *busy*, here, refers to a gathering of at least two or three people.

Instead of following a routine of proper recitation and meditation, their recitation will become like idle chatter, empty and fruitless words. They will also constantly disparage those who are engaged in hearing and reflection, stating that such practices are not true Dharma and therefore unnecessary. And towards good meditators they feel jealous.

> Their own meditation is nothing but distraction.
> Give up meditation based on the eight worldly concerns!

When we speak of meditation, we refer to a state of mind that is free of distraction and free of the two hindrances of mental sinking and agitation. The mind of those who are preoccupied with concerns of this life, however, is instead free of mindfulness and awareness. This means that it will be either sinking and dull, or distracted and agitated, unable to remain with the object of meditation. These are clear indications that our meditation is based on the eight worldly concerns. Since such practice is of no real benefit, we would do well to drop it straight away.

The Second Line:
"If You Are Attached To Saṃsāra, You Have No Renunciation."

Introduction

We will now turn to the second line of the instructions:

> If you are attached to saṃsāra, you have no renunciation.

If it is our goal to attain buddhahood, we have to recognize that our own situation as well as the whole of saṃsāra as riddled with flaws and generate a sense of revulsion towards it to overcome our attachment. If we do not see saṃsāra as a problem, the wish to go beyond it and to achieve something else will not arise, just as the wish to replace some equipment we own will arise only when we know for sure that it is broken or outdated. As long as it is working well, there is no need to look for something else.

To generate the needed sense of revulsion, we contemplate the faults of saṃsāra. For this we must first hear the explanations of these flaws and study them well, and then deeply reflect on them repeatedly. If we only hear about them once, it might help us arouse a little distaste, but there will be no lasting benefit. When it rains on a stone, the water does not penetrate its core and so it will quickly dry as soon as it stops raining. In a similar way, listening to a lecture about the flaws of saṃsāra once will not be of great benefit. We should reflect on these points many times and familiarize our mind with them until there is a change of perspective in us and we have a general outlook in life that is imbued with the wish to get out of saṃsāra.

I. A General Assessment of Saṃsāra

To discuss the faults of saṃsāra, we will first look at saṃsāra as a whole to understand what the general problem is. After this, we will investigate the various specific forms of suffering that afflict sentient beings.

The countless forms of suffering and dissatisfaction of saṃsāra are inconceivable, but they can be subsumed in various ways: the three categories of suffering, the eight types of suffering, or the six types of suffering.

A. The Three Categories of Suffering

The term *suffering* itself is not that easy to understand. It comprises three broad categories of suffering: the suffering of suffering, the suffering of change, and the pervasive suffering of conditioned existence. *Suffering of suffering* denotes all painful or distressing sensations of body and mind, together with the mind and mental factors arising together with these feelings, as well as the objects—i.e., the defiled phenomena—which function as a support for them to arise. *Suffering of change* indicates all pleasant sensations of body and mind, along with the associated mind, mental factors, and defiled objects. *Pervasive suffering of conditioned existence* comprises all neutral sensations which are neither pleasant nor suffering, as well as the mind, mental factors, and defiled objects associated with these sensations. This is how these three categories of sufferings are explained in the Abhidharma.

The great Dharmakīrti defines the pervasive suffering of conditioned existence as all defiled states and phenomena that arise on the basis of karma and mental afflictions. The term *defiled* indicates all phenomena, on the basis of which mental afflictions can arise and develop.

The meditation manuals, such as those of the Lamdré tradition, teach the same three categories of suffering, albeit presented in a different way. There, *suffering of suffering* refers to the suffering of the three lower realms, *suffering of change* to the suffering of the higher realms, such as the rich becoming poor, and the *pervasive suffering of conditioned existence* is identified as the fact that our worldly activities just never come to an end.

B. The Eight Types of Suffering

The first of the eight types of suffering is the *suffering of birth*, which indicates the intense suffering experienced by a being in the mother's womb and during the process of birth itself. The second is the *suffering of old age*, which can have many forms, such as the loss of youth's beauty and the decline of physical, verbal, and mental strength. Even if one remains healthy, the process of ageing entails many forms of suffering. Third is the *suffering of sickness*, which includes all kinds of diseases and all the hardships endured in the process of trying to cure them, such as surgeries, as well as the mental suffering that comes with this, such as the stress experienced by spending one's savings for treatment and so forth. Fourth is the *suffering of death*, which refers to the many difficult experiences associated with the dying process. When the time comes to give up this beloved body and everything they hold dear, ordinary beings are overwhelmed by intense mental distress. Moreover, those who have committed severe negative deeds will be tormented by visions of the hell realms, and those who have even a little understanding of the Dharma but missed the opportunity to put it into practice will be overwhelmed by great regret.

Fifth is the *suffering of encountering enemies and hostility*. This can relate to individual people, groups, or countries, with which a mere encounter brings about any form of physical or mental harm or stress. Sixth is the *suffering of being separated from one's beloved and dear ones*, that is, one's parents, relatives, friends, and so forth, from whom temporary and in particular final separation generates unbearable sorrow and pain. Seventh is the *suffering of not being able to fulfill one's wishes*, such as a businessperson not being able to generate the desired profit. This also occurs when someone places their hopes in another person to accomplish their spiritual or worldly aims and their wishes are not fulfilled; this can generate severe stress and anxiety. In brief, it is the mental suffering we experience every time our wishes are not fulfilled, or our expectations are not met.

The last of the eight types of suffering is described as follows in the scriptures: "In brief, *the five skandhas of clinging are suffering*." The skandhas of clinging comprise all the components of our body and our mind. Since they function as the basis for the other afflictions and for suffering to arise, their nature is that of the pervasive suffering of conditioned existence.

C. The Six Types of Suffering

When we speak of the six types of suffering, the first is the uncertainty of friends and foes. The second is the fact that our desires are never quenched: whatever we eat or drink, whatever possessions we own, we always want more. Similarly, regardless of how many times they have engaged in acts of sexual copulation, beings are never satisfied. Third, the continuous discarding of bodies: since there is no beginning to our existence in saṃsāra, we have had countless lives, and each time we had to discard our body. Fourth, the continuous need to take up a new body: as long as they are bound by the shackles of karma and afflictions, beings have no choice but to continuously take birth in saṃsāra, life after life after life. Fifth, the suffering of uncertain status: those who enjoy a high position fall to a lower rank, the rich become poor, and so forth. Lastly, the sixth is the suffering of being utterly alone at the time of death: no one will accompany us on this journey.

II. THE SPECIFIC SUFFERINGS OF SENTIENT BEINGS

A. The Suffering of Beings in the Hell Realm

Sentient beings undergo a variety of sufferings depending on their individual conditions. Among these, we will first discuss the conditions experienced by beings in the cold hells. Their outer environment consists of snow mountains and frozen plains where snow constantly falls. Beings there have nothing to wear and no housing or shelter of any kind. It is a very dark and gloomy place. There are eight such cold hells:

(1) In the Hell of Blisters, the cold is so intense that the entire body of beings there is covered in blisters. (2) In Hell of Bursting Blisters, it is so cold that the blisters crack and turn into open wounds. (3) In the Hell of Cries, the cold is so great that one loses all self-control only to cry out in pain "So cold!" (4) In the Hell of Laments, one's voice is reduced to pitiful whispers, helplessly lamenting "Oh my!" and the like. (5) In

the Hell of Chattering Teeth, one is no longer able to emit any sound due to the extreme cold; the body shivers and the teeth chatter. (6) In the Hell Split Open Like an Utpala Flower, the entire body turns blue like an utpala flower and splits into many pieces. (7) In the Hell Split Open Like a Lotus, the body becomes red like a lotus and cracks into even more pieces. (8) In the Hell Greatly Split Open Like a Lotus, the extreme cold burns not only skin and flesh, but also the internal organs, which turn red and also crack into many pieces.

If we humans were to experience, even for just one minute, the pain endured in these hell realms, we would die instantly. However, due to the force of their karma, these beings cannot die but must undergo such agonies for a very long time.

The first of the eight hot hells is called (1) Reviving Hell. Having taken birth there miraculously, the beings in this environment see each other only as enemies. They spontaneously hold weapons in their hands with which they attack and kill each other. However, they do not really die but merely faint for a while, only to be revived and go through the same experience of killing each other again. This is the kind of suffering beings undergo in this hell. (2) In the Black Line Hell, the minions of hell draw black lines on the beings' bodies, hack them up with axes, and chop them into pieces. (3) The beings in the Crushing Hell are chased by the guardians of hell between mountains that resemble animal heads. Trapped and crushed between these mountains, they suffer terrible wounds with blood oozing out of them. (4) In the Screaming Hell, beings are burned alive in iron houses without doors in which great fires rage, and so they scream terribly. (5) In the Great Screaming Hell, the space they are confined to consists of two houses, one within the other, and so their suffering is greater still. (6 and 7) In the hells of Heat and Extreme Heat, beings are impaled on three-pointed iron stakes and badly beaten. (8) In the Hell of

Unceasing Torment, the suffering is the most intense. At this point, the fires of hell and the beings' bodies can no longer be distinguished and so they suffer the greatest possible pain. Generally, the sufferings of the beings in the hot hells are manifold. They must eat pieces of burning steel and drink molten iron. Some are tied onto burning iron wheels and others are bound with burning iron chains.

To each of the four sides outside the eight hot hells are four neighboring hells, each characterized by a specific form of suffering. Thus, there are sixteen such neighboring hells in total. The first of these is the Hell of Burning Embers, where beings fall into pits of embers, burning the skin of their bodies and roasting their flesh. In the Swamp of Putrid Corpses, they sink into swamps of rotting bodies emitting a disgusting stench and filled with maggots that bore into one's flesh. The third neighboring hell is the Roads of Blades where beings are tormented with weapons. The paths there are paved with upright razor-sharp blades that slice one's feet with every step one takes. As one lifts one's foot it instantly heals, only to be sliced again with the next step. The forest in this hell is the Jungle of Leaves of Swords, where dangerous weapons constantly fall on the beings there, causing unimaginable suffering. Lastly, there is the Mountain of Weapons, also called the Śālmalī Stalks. When the beings who have engaged in sexual misconduct, as well as those who have excessive attachment to sensual pleasures, are born there, they see the objects of their attachment at the foot of the mountain. They rush there to be united with them, but as soon as they reach that place there appears a massive dog that ferociously attacks and savages them. As they try to climb the mountain, the blades of the stalks all point downward, cutting their bodies everywhere. They then see the objects of their desire at the top of the mountain, but as soon as they arrive there, they are nowhere to be seen. Instead, they are welcomed by a massive bird that attacks them, pecking through their skull and jabbing at their eyes. The objects of attachment then again appear at the bottom of the mountain. As they descend, the blades all point towards them, and so they again suffer terribly on their way down.

There are also so-called occasional hells, where the suffering is the least intense among all the hells. These are located anywhere in the hells and also in the human realm. Beings in these states may experience comfort during the day and suffer greatly at night.

B. The Suffering of Hungry Ghosts

There are three different types of hungry ghosts. The four main types of suffering that torment all of them are: the suffering of hunger and thirst; the suffering of great fear, such as the terror they experience at the sight of armed guards; the physical hardships they undergo in search of food, with their weak bodies and having to travel great distances; and the heat and cold they endure: in the winter even the sun intensifies the cold, and in the summer even the moonlight is hot. These are the four general types of suffering all hungry ghosts experience.

Regarding the three types of hungry ghosts, the first suffer from being denied access to any food they may see by armed guards. The second type of hungry ghosts, though not stopped by others from eating, faces other hardships. They are utterly malnourished, their mouth is smaller than the eye of a needle, their throat is as small as a single hair, their belly is as large as an empty valley, and their legs are like twigs. Whatever scraps of food they find are dirty and disgusting, and due to their habituation to miserliness, they do not immediately eat what they find but stingily keep it for later. Whatever they then end up eating does not fit into their tiny mouth, and even if it does, the food does not pass through their throat. Whatever ends up in their stomach does not nourish them or satisfy their hunger in the least due to the enormous size of their belly. The third type of hungry ghosts suffers moreover from a fire blazing in their stomach whenever they consume the smallest amount of food.

When these hungry ghosts see fruit trees, just their looking at them causes all the fruit to shrivel and dry up. Some cause entire rivers to dry out the moment they see them, others turn them into rivers of pus. The cause for being born as a hungry ghost is miserliness, as discussed earlier during the explanation of the karmic law of cause and result.

C. The Suffering of Animals

Most animals live in the oceans and those sea creatures are of many types. Generally speaking, all of them must endure numerous kinds of suffering, such as constant uncertainty as to the beings they share their space with. Additionally, they also experience particular forms of suffering, such as certain animals devouring each other, large groups of small animals being eaten alive by large ones, and single large ones being attacked and eaten by many small ones.

Other animals live scattered among the humans and gods. Among those some, like deer, for example, live in constant anguish and fear. As the saying goes, "Most humans are miserable, most dogs are hungry, and most deer are filled with fear."

Most animals owned by humans are forced to work hard, only to be slaughtered in the end. Innumerable animals are farmed and kept alive for the sole purpose of being killed to collect their flesh, their fur, or their skin. And while trapped in their enclosures, they end up fighting amongst each other.

Many have no home or shelter in which to seek refuge and they have no weapons to protect themselves. Since animal flesh is generally the favorite food of humans, they have to endure so much hardship and suffering. All this is fairly obvious.

D. The Suffering of Humans

The sufferings experienced by humans are similar in nature to those of the other five classes of beings. Like hell beings, humans endure heat and cold, are killed, mutilated, and burned alive. Like hungry ghosts, they suffer from hunger and thirst. Like animals, humans are dominated by others, exploited by the powerful and forced to work for them. Like asuras, they also experience the suffering of conflict and strife, whether it is individuals fighting with each other or nations waging war. Lastly, like the gods, humans suffer from losing whatever privileged or esteemed position they temporarily hold.

Moreover, those who possess great wealth and enjoy a certain social standing have a lot of stress and mental suffering, and those who are destitute face a great number of physical and material hardships. Suffering is truly everywhere! Those who have a short life suffer from this particular predicament, and those who have a long life suffer from the ailments of old age. The poor see their condition as a source of great problems, but the rich also face their own share of hardship and misery, since every possession contaminated by mental afflictions brings with it suffering and negativity. When many people live together, there is more trouble, and when there are few, we suffer from lack of companions.

Even the simple acts of walking or sitting are in the nature of suffering. When we walk too much, for instance, sitting down makes us happy. But this is not true happiness: it is merely the fact that we have substituted one suffering for another that gives us the impression that it is something pleasant. If sitting would bring about true happiness, the more we sat, the happier we would be. However, sitting for extended periods of time produces discomfort and pain. The same is true for walking.

Furthermore, we go to great lengths to avoid suffering and this alone keeps us very busy. For example, the food we consume does not satisfy us for long; we will feel hungry just two or three hours after a meal. Even the very act of eating can cause a lot of problems. When we are hot or cold, we have to regulate these conditions by wearing appropriate clothing, which is another source of trouble. Basically, we are constantly occupied with activities which have as their sole purpose avoiding or regulating all kinds of sufferings.

In brief, no matter how happy we may be, "compounded phenomena are not beyond the four endings." This means that compounded phenomena cannot go beyond the limitations imposed by the four types of ending: (1) birth ends in death; (2) meeting ends in separation; (3) accumulation ends in exhaustion—whatever wealth one may acquire, it will eventually all be used up; and (4) building ends in collapse—everything we build, including our houses, will one day collapse.

E. The Suffering of the Gods

Two types of gods can generally be distinguished. The first live in abundance and have everything they desire—far more than we humans could ever possess—which brings them a lot of pleasure. However, they still encounter a great number of difficulties, since the asuras are constantly fighting them for their wealth and prosperity. Others live in poverty, possessing nothing but the clothes on their back, and struggle in this way. One major source of suffering for these gods is the death process. Ten different signs announce their imminent demise: their bodies becoming unattractive, the flower garlands they wear wither, etc. When these signs are observed by companions, the dying one is immediately abandoned. As a gesture of farewell, they throw flowers from afar and then leave to join their other friends and companions. Seeing this, the gods who are about to die understand that their time has come. This causes them excruciating mental suffering. It is said that this mental agony is greater even than the physical pain endured by the beings in the hell realm, and it does not end after just a few days. Counted in human years, this kind of hardship would last for many thousands of years.

The beings of the two higher realms of existence are also referred to as gods. Even though these gods do not experience any overt suffering, they carry the seeds of unwholesome deeds in their mindstream, leading them to be reborn in the lower realms after their godly existence. When our teacher, the Buddha, was asked, "What are the faults of saṃsāra?" he replied, "The problem with cyclic existence is twofold: suffering and impermanence." These words perfectly summarize the condition of saṃsāra. Suffering is what beings do not want, and impermanence is what they call happiness. This happiness, however, is not permanent.

III. The Benefits of Contemplating the Suffering of Saṃsāra

Why is it important for us to consider all these sufferings? It is not the case that certain kinds of suffering are reserved for certain beings and that others are exempt from them. The sufferings beings undergo are the result of the negative deeds they have accumulated since time without beginning, and they are experienced individually by those who have committed these deeds. This will continue for countless, immeasurable eons until they attain liberation. Saṃsāra truly is like a prison, where beings, like prisoners, are bound with the shackles of mental afflictions, causing endless suffering. This is how we ought to think of saṃsāra. A prisoner has only one thought: "How can I gain my freedom?" Likewise, we should also think, "I must get out of saṃsāra; I must put it down. I have to gain liberation from cyclic existence, once and for all!" This is the thought of renunciation.

No one is attached to the suffering of saṃsāra, not even animals. However, deluded as they are about the pleasures and delights of saṃsāra, beings relish it. This is why these pleasures need to be abandoned. The prosperity and the joys of saṃsāra are like poisonous fruits: delicious to the taste, but harmful for one's health. Being attached to them is like taking the offspring of a demon as one's spouse: they may please us at first, but they will kill us eventually. In a forest fire, birds are quick to escape for fear of being harmed by the flames. We should have a similar attitude with regard to saṃsāra: terrified of all its suffering, we wish nothing but to be free.

Nāgārjuna stated that if someone's hair and clothes caught fire, they would immediately cease all other activities to extinguish the flames. Even more important than stopping such fires, he added, is to engage in the means of liberation. This means that, rather than being concerned with our body and our life, we should devote ourselves entirely to the path that leads to liberation from saṃsāra.

A reminder on the right motivation for teaching and receiving the Dharma

Teachers of the Dharma should have the right motivation when they expound the doctrine, and their explanations should be free of faults. As for the listeners, they should approach the teachings with the intention to rid themselves of mental afflictions. Considering that the purpose of the Dharma they receive is to attain buddhahood to benefit others, they should make every effort and listen carefully. In this way, both the teacher and the listener generate extraordinary merit, far greater than that accrued by any other good deed. It is said that not only do the actions of teaching and listening based on such motivations constitute the path of the Mahāyāna, but simply breathing in or taking a single step in order to be able to teach or listen to the Dharma in this way produces great merit.

IV. Supplementary Teachings

A. Afflictions, Mind, and Mental Factors

When we explained the causes and results of saṃsāra, we talked about the causes mainly in terms of karma or actions, and about the result in terms of the various states of existence of saṃsāra. However, we should understand that mental afflictions are more important in this regard than the actions themselves. Why is this so? Because it is solely due to mental afflictions that sentient beings keep roaming in saṃsāra. Beings are born in the hell realm due to anger, whereas actions by themselves, if they are not associated with mental afflictions, are unable to produce suffering. Reflecting in this way on the causes and conditions that bring about birth in saṃsāra, we understand that the main causes are our mental afflictions. It is therefore of utmost importance that we be very cautious and pay close attention to the afflictions in our mind. I will therefore take this opportunity to explain them a bit here.

A mental affliction is a mental event that agitates the mind, making it unpeaceful. There are many kinds of mental afflictions, but the most important ones can be subsumed into the six root afflictions and the twenty secondary afflictions. The six root afflictions are desire, hatred, ignorance, pride, doubt, and afflicted views. The first three have been explained earlier. Pride means to think or feel that one is superior to others. Doubt is defined as a mental state that harbors uncertainty with regard to the truth of the karmic law of cause and result and the four truths. In other words, not every doubt is a mental affliction. To be uncertain about tomorrow's weather, for instance, is not.

The sixth root affliction is afflicted views. An afflicted view is a mind that misapprehends its object, viewing it in a way that is not in agreement with or is in contradiction to its true nature. Afflicted views are subdivided into five kinds, the first is which is called the view of the perishing collection, which is nothing other than self-grasping. Thus, the five views are counted as one in the list of the six root afflictions.

The secondary afflictions are derived from the root afflictions and are slightly less powerful or intense. They include jealousy, which is a mind of aversion or dislike regarding another's good fortune or positive qualities; stinginess, which occurs when the mind strongly clings to one's own outer or inner possessions; laziness, such as the lack of interest in accomplishing wholesome deeds; and many others.

How do these afflictions and actions produce birth in saṃsāra? This occurs in a gradual manner. First is the self-grasping present in our mindstream; this is the root of saṃsāra. The afflictions that arise from this are the causes for an individual to be continuously reborn in saṃsāra. The actions motivated by these afflictions provide the conditions for these births. The relationship between causes and conditions can be illustrated by the analogy of a flower. The seed of the flower is the cause and the water, the soil, and so forth are the conditions.

To elaborate further on this process, we can say that the thought "I" arises in dependence on an individual's body, the sensations they experience, and their mind. This is called self-grasping. When there is grasping of an "I," grasping of "other" will naturally arise in dependence on that. Due to this, there will be attachment to "I" and aversion to "other," and based on these two impulses, many other afflictions, such as pride, will arise. In dependence on these afflictions, the individual will engage in all kinds of actions. In this way, it is in dependence on afflictions and actions that the various births among the five or six types of beings are established.

All afflictions fall under the category of mental factors. Since some students have not had the opportunity to study the philosophical treatises, I would like to expound a bit on this subject. Generally, we distinguish between the mind and the mental factors, where mind refers to the principal element of cognition and the mental factors to its retinue. This distinction is based on their different modes of perception. The mind is that which apprehends what is called the mere object, that is, it perceives an object in terms of its essential nature. The mental factors apprehend the object's distinctive features, that is, they perceive an object in terms of its specific features, such as whether an object is perceived as beautiful or ugly, and so forth.

The Hīnayāna schools speak of six different types of main mind. According to the Mahāyāna tradition, however, there are eight. That which, based on the visual sense faculty, perceives forms in terms of shapes and colors is the eye consciousness. That which, based on the auditory sense faculty, perceives sounds is the ear consciousness. Similarly, that which perceives smells based on the olfactory sense faculty is the nose consciousness; that which perceives tastes based on the gustatory sense faculty is the tongue consciousness; and that which perceives objects of touch, such as softness or roughness, based on the tactile sense faculty is the body consciousness. The sixth consciousness is the mental consciousness. It is this one which apprehends all kinds of objects of the past, present, or future and which thinks all kinds of thoughts. These six types of consciousness occur when the necessary causes and conditions come together. When the causes and conditions are incomplete, they stop, such as in the state of deep sleep.

The seventh consciousness is the afflicted mind. This is the mind that is focused on the universal ground consciousness and apprehends it as "I." In other words, it is the notion of identity based on the universal ground consciousness. In ordinary beings, this afflicted mind continues without interruption. The question of whether it is present even in the state of deep sleep is debated among scholars.

The eighth is the universal ground consciousness. It is receptive to all types of objects, meaning it does not have a specific kind of object, such as form or sound. However, its mode of perception is devoid of clarity. This means that the universal ground consciousness does not apprehend its objects clearly. This mind also continues without interruption, from time without beginning until buddhahood is attained, and it carries the latencies of all actions accumulated, whether wholesome or unwholesome. When it is pointed out, it is explained to be the mere luminosity of the present awareness, the knowing before it engages with objects. This is the universal ground consciousness.

Mental factors are expressions of the mind. They are the various ways in which the mind apprehends objects. This can be illustrated with the analogy of the ocean: the mind is like the ocean and the mental factors are like its waves. According to the higher Indian Buddhist tenet systems, mind and mental factors are of one nature. Even though there is a wide variety of mental factors, they all are subsumed into the fifty-one principal mental factors in the Mahāyāna Abhidharma system. As mentioned earlier, they include all mental afflictions, such as desire or hatred, but also the wholesome states, such as faith, the mental state of taking refuge, love, compassion, diligence, and so forth.

B. The Twelve Links of Dependent Arising

One subject crucial for the understanding of saṃsāra and nirvāṇa is the twelve links of dependent arising. When this is well understood, we will appreciate how karma and afflictions cause sentient beings to roam in saṃsāra and how saṃsāra can be overcome in dependence on the practice of the path.

The first of the twelve links is ignorance. Here, ignorance does not refer to the delusion of the three root poisons, but specifically to self-grasping. What is the difference? Delusion does not have the ability to induce wholesome deeds, whereas self-grasping does. If these two were the same, then all actions accumulated on the basis of self-grasping would be unwholesome, which is not the case.

The second link is formations, which denotes karma or actions. Actions are of three kinds: wholesome, unwholesome, and those that produce rebirth in the higher realms of saṃsāra.

Third is consciousness. Ārya Nāgārjuna explains that this link specifically designates consciousness when it first enters the mother's womb.

Fourth is name-and-form. Of the five skandhas that comprise a sentient being, sensation, perception, formative factors, and consciousness are subsumed under the term *name*. *Form* denotes the body that initially forms in the mother's womb, which begins as an oval-shaped embryo.[1]

Fifth are the six sense bases: the eyes, ears, nose, and tongue, together with the two earlier ones, body and mind.

Sixth is the mental factor of contact, which is the apprehension of the distinctive features of the objects of perception, perceiving things in terms of "good" and "bad," and so forth.

Seventh is the mental factor of sensation, which is the experience of pleasure and pain, etc.

Eighth is the mental factor of craving, which manifests, for instance, as the desire not to be separated from pleasure or as the wish to be free of suffering.

Ninth is the mental factor of clinging, such as the attachment to the source of pleasure or the wish to obtain it.

Tenth is becoming, which again refers to karma, or actions. Generally, karma is of two types. The first type are actions, whether newly committed or performed in the past, that have not yet produced their karmic results. The second type are actions motivated by craving and clinging, which give rise to strong desire. Such actions reinforce the potential of the first type of deeds and therefore can produce their results in later births. This second type of action is referred to as "becoming."

Eleventh is birth, which denotes the birth of the being itself with its skandhas.

Lastly, the twelfth link is aging-and-death, which are counted together.

Of these twelve links, the first, the eighth, and the ninth (i.e., ignorance, craving, and clinging) are mental afflictions; the second and the tenth (i.e., formations and becoming) are karma; and the remaining seven are their result of full maturation.

The twelve links are also explained in terms of causes and results stretching over the course of three lifetimes. In this case, ignorance and formations belong to a past birth, the eight links from consciousness to becoming belong to the middle life, and birth and aging-and-death belong to later existence. In this way, the twelve links can be completed within three lifetimes when the process unfolds quickly. In terms of causes and results, the ignorance and formations of the past life function as the causes for the middle life's next five links of consciousness, and so forth. The middle life's craving, clinging, and becoming then establish the causes for the two results, which are the birth and aging-and-death of the third life.

C. Contemplating the Faults of the Afflictions

We shall now consider the faults of the afflictions. In his *Ornament of the Mahāyāna Sūtras*, Ārya Maitreya gives a concise explanation, stating that every single mental affliction, be it desire, hatred, or any other, does nothing but harm oneself and others, as well as impair our roots of goodness. Under the influence of afflictions, our ethical conduct declines, and we engage in actions that we will later regret and for which others will despise us. These are just some of their faults.

In *The Way of the Bodhisattva*, Śāntideva explains that while afflictions are like enemies, in that both inflict harm upon us, afflictions are infinitely worse. While ordinary enemies can only hurt us for a short period of time, the afflictive emotions in our mind have abused us incessantly since time without beginning, and they will continue to harm us for endless time to come. Even if every single being in the world became our enemy, they could only ever injure us in this life. Afflictions, however, are enemies that can lead us to the realms of hell. If we relate to our ordinary enemies respectfully, with the intention of being helpful and beneficial to them, they will not harm us in return. But our afflictions only get worse the more we follow them and comply with their demands. Even if we are utterly helpless and unable to defend ourselves, our ordinary enemies will, at some point, die by themselves. Our mental afflictions, however, will never cede on their own accord: they will only cease once we conquer them through the application of antidotes.

With these and other reflections, Śāntideva clearly explains why it is of utmost importance to be very vigilant and cautious regarding the afflictions present in our mind.

D. The Wheel of Becoming

I thought it would be beneficial at this point to briefly explain the meaning of the images of the so-called wheel of becoming, as this illustration captures the basics of Buddhadharma. It symbolizes the processes of saṃsāra and nirvāṇa. In the scriptures of the greater and the lesser vehicles, they are formulated in terms of the four truths—a subject that must be well understood. The four truths comprise the causal and the resultant aspects of both saṃsāra and liberation. The causes of saṃsāra are karma and afflictions, the result of which is saṃsāra, which means the outer environments and the beings living in them. The causal and resultant aspects of liberation are, in simple terms, the qualities in the mind of the Dharma practitioner, such as the eightfold path of the noble ones—i.e, the "truth of the path"—and the freedom from mental afflictions and the suffering they produce, i.e., the "truth of cessation."

In the center of the wheel of becoming we can see three animals. These symbolize the causes of saṃsāra, in other words, the origin of suffering. The pig symbolizes delusion, the snake hatred, and the bird desire. In the circle around them are depictions of the three lower realms and the realms of the gods and humans. These represent the truth of suffering. In the outer rim we find drawings of the twelve links of dependent arising.

They explain in terms of cause and result how beings roam in saṃsāra.[2]

To the right above the wheel are two verses spoken by the Buddha, symbolizing the truth of the path, and above them is a moon, which represents the truth of cessation. To the left of the wheel is a drawing of the Buddha standing and pointing at both the moon and the wheel. This represents that we should pay close attention to the path to liberation and its result.

This completes my short explanation of the second line of the instructions on Parting from the Four Attachments: "If you are attached to saṃsāra, you have no renunciation."

The Third Line:
"If You Are Attached to Your Own Self-Interest, You Have No Bodhicitta."

Introduction

We will now discuss the meaning of the third line: "If you are attached to your own self-interest, you have no bodhicitta." Even though saṃsāra seems to have certain benefits for us, there really are none. The Buddha clearly explained how it is in fact riddled with serious flaws and shortcomings. We should be skilled at investigating saṃsāra in terms of its general and particular faults, as previously explained. In this way, we will recognize that saṃsāra is something to be abandoned, and we will let go of all attachment to it and look for a method to free ourselves from it once and for all.

What are we to do once the sincere wish to be free of saṃsāra has been born? There are two possibilities: following the path that leads to the level of a Hīnayāna arhat, or applying the methods that lead to the perfect awakening of a buddha. Even though the former is a truly great accomplishment, the achievement of complete buddhahood is a much greater one still. Based on this reflection, generating the wish to accomplish this most exalted level is what is called the Mahāyāna resolve for awakening.

It is important that we ask ourselves: "What do I want to accomplish? What is my aim?" Based on our answers, we can then also formulate clear intentions like: "I must attain this aim in this life," or "In my future life, I must attain a human life or be born as a god and avoid the lower realms," or "I must attain liberation," or "I must accomplish buddhahood." We should use whichever of these formulations inspires us most and practice them diligently. In the end, the most important point is to follow the practice that has the greatest beneficial impact on us.

I. Cultivating Altruistic Love

A. *The Cause of Aspiring and Engaging Bodhicitta*

Even though the Mahāyāna resolve for awakening has many divisions, from the point of view of their nature, two types are taught: aspiring bodhicitta and engaging bodhicitta. Aspiring bodhicitta is the wish to attain buddhahood for the benefit of others. There is no tradition of generating the resolve for awakening for one's own benefit in the Mahāyāna. Engaging bodhicitta is the resolve to engage in the wholesome actions that are the causes of buddhahood in order to attain this goal.

To generate this twofold bodhicitta in one's mindstream, all the causes and conditions must be complete. Of the many causes of bodhicitta, compassion is the most important. This is why it must be cultivated well as a preliminary step for the generation of bodhicitta. The cause of compassion, in turn, is altruistic love. This means that this altruism needs to be cultivated first.

Altruism is the wish for others to enjoy a well-being and a happiness that is in harmony with the Dharma, in this life and in their future lives, until they attain the supreme happiness of buddhahood. This also includes the wish to assist them in accomplishing the wholesome deeds that are the causes of happiness. This level of altruism is not naturally present in new Dharma practitioners and must be generated and developed.

Generally speaking, we can say that to practice the Dharma means to actively work with the mind in a wholesome way, to turn the mind into something good. Our mind is like pure gold: it can be formed and shaped into anything we want. The result of not having done this work in the past is that our mind now contains many shortcomings. All of these faults are located in the mind and originate in the mind. When these shortcomings are addressed and worked with through the practice of Dharma, the mind will transform, up to a point when it will be replete with many qualities. All these qualities have their origin in the mind itself. In other words, the mind has the ability to change into whatever it is accustomed to.

In terms of how this transformation is achieved, we should not be satisfied with the knowledge of the Dharma acquired through hearing and contemplation alone. The things we learn must transform our attitude and change the mind from the inside. For this to happen, we must allow the mind to be infused and merge with these states. This is achieved by putting forth effort in repeating this process of familiarization over and over again, without allowing the mind to wander off into dullness or distraction.

B. The Benefits of Cultivating Altruistic Love

It is said that the merit gained from cultivating altruistic concern for just a few minutes is greater than that earned by offering countless beautiful and pleasing gifts to many buddhas over a long period of time. The teachings mention that by meditating on altruism, or love, for the time it would take to milk a cow, we obtain eight different benefits, such as being cared for by gods and humans. It is evident that if we take care of others, others will take care of us in return. This is called "the result that is similar to the cause." Not only that: an altruistic mind has the power to protect ourself and others from harm. When our teacher the Buddha was assaulted and attacked by many māras, it was the power of his altruistic love that made it impossible for them to harm him. Further, to attain buddhahood, we require compassion, which, in turn, requires the presence of a genuine altruistic concern.

C. How to Cultivate Love

When we first meditate on love, that is, when we begin to familiarize the mind with this quality of altruistic concern, we should cultivate it in three steps: first towards those close to us, then towards those we perceive as enemies, and finally towards all others, who are neither our friends nor our enemies.

1. Altruistic love for those close to us

This first step also entails three stages: love for our mother; love for those who have been particularly kind to us, like our father; and love for other relatives and friends with whom we have good relations. Later on, we cultivate love for all beings, considering that every being has been our mother in the past. Why do we cultivate altruistic love in this way? Because it is easiest to first generate and deepen our love for those we already genuinely care for. Our mother holds a very special place in our heart, as do our children and our partner. For those with whom we share such special bonds, thoughts of kindness and the wish for them not to suffer will naturally arise in us. We don't need to make special efforts for this. It is therefore the simplest way to generate love and compassion in our mindstream.

a. Love for our mother

We begin by identifying our own mother as the object of our compassion. Then, we reflect on the great kindness she has shown us. Finally, we generate the intention to repay her kindness. By following this procedure, we will be able to generate genuine altruistic love.

i. Thinking of one's mother

Whether our mother is still alive or has passed, we begin by thinking that she is right there in front of us, visualizing her physical features, just as she is or was. We concentrate on the visual image in front and think: "This is my kind mother." We can also say these words out loud a couple of times.

ii. Recalling her great kindness

Then, we continue by concentrating with focused attention on our visualized mother and think of the various ways she cared for us and how kind she was to us. A mother's kindness can be summarized in three points: (1) the kindness of giving us this body and life; (2) the kindness of instructing and educating us in many ways; and (3) the kindness of undergoing many challenges and hardships for our sake.

For nine months, she carried us in her womb, guarding us with great care. When we were born, our body was incapable of doing anything on its own, we were unable to speak, and even our mind could not think in any meaningful way. Our mother, however, took such great care of us: she fed us when we were hungry and gave us to drink when we were thirsty; she made sure that we are never too hot nor too cold, and she always protected us from any danger. In this way, our mother gave us this very body and life.

As we grew up, she educated us in many ways, teaching us words like "mama," showing us how to walk, how to sit, how to eat and drink, and so forth. When we were a bit older and more independent, she offered us her belongings, which could have taken her a long time to gather. She probably underwent lots of hardships to acquire them and might even have committed serious misdeeds in the process, just to be able to provide us with something. She could have benefited her own future lives by using her wealth for the sake of Dharma, or she could have enjoyed it in this life for her own pleasure. Instead, she sacrificed her own well-being and gave it to us, her child, without second thought. In brief, mothers benefit their children in every way they can and know, and they protect them from all kinds of harm and difficulties. We should deeply reflect on these aspects of our mother's kindness.

When we recall our mother's kindness, we should also consider that our mother has cared for us not only in this life. She has been our mother countless times in our past lives, and every time she benefited us in all these ways. Similarly, she was our father, our relatives, and our dear friends innumerable times, benefiting us in many ways, caring for us with great love and affection. We should also recall her kindness in this way and deeply reflect on it.

iii. Wishing to repay her kindness

After contemplating her kindness, we generate the wish to repay our mother's kindness. For this, we should think: "My mother has been so incredibly kind to me. I must repay her kindness." Then, we should examine our mother's present condition: "Even though she wishes to be happy, she does not deeply understand how wholesome deeds are the causes of happiness and therefore engages in negative deeds. She might even kill, steal, or lie in search of happiness, thus effectively accumulating the causes of suffering. This is why she is still not able to accomplish her own well-being. I must help her."

iv. Four methods of practice

When we generate the thought "I wish for my mother to be happy and that she engages in wholesome deeds, the causes of happiness," it is called the cultivation of love associated with a wish. When we think "May my mother have happiness and the causes of happiness, wholesome deeds," it is the cultivation of love associated with aspiration. To think "May the lama and the Three Jewels help my mother gain happiness and the causes of happiness" is called the cultivation of love associated with prayer. Similarly, when we think "I will make it possible for my mother to enjoy happiness and the causes of happiness," it is called the cultivation of love associated with the promise of bodhicitta.

We should use whichever of these four methods works best for us until this altruistic love for our mother is genuine and natural. Sometimes we first contemplate the causes that give rise to love and then cultivate altruism based on these four methods, and sometimes we simply familiarize ourselves with the mind of love with the help of these words, without reflecting on its causes. By practicing in this way continuously for a week or a month, during our formal meditation sessions as well as during post-meditation, the wish for our mother to be truly happy and to have the causes of happiness will be continuously on our minds without having to generate it with deliberate effort. At this point, genuine altruistic love for our mother has reached full maturity.

b. Love for our dear ones

To cultivate love for others who are very dear to us, like our father, we follow the same method as just explained. We first reflect on how they have benefited us in this life. Then, we consider how, in previous lives, they have been our mothers many times, each time helping us in countless ways, as described above. In this way, genuine love for them will be born in us.

c. Love for others with whom we have good relations

Here, we again follow the same procedure of reflection and meditation, as it was explained above.

2. Love for enemies

Next, it is important to extend our love to our enemies as well. From a purely worldly perspective, we cannot say that enemies benefit us in this life. Here, however, instead of thinking only about the harm they caused us and what they did, and getting upset and angry as a result, we should find a way to generate love and the intention to benefit them in response to their deeds. Why? Because even those we now perceive as enemies have been our mothers many times in previous lives, and every time they cared for us with the same kindness we have received from the mother of our present life. Therefore, we should think "I must repay her kindness!" and bring forth a love for our enemies that is equal to the love we have for our mother and familiarize our mind with it.

3. Love for all beings

For this third step, we think that all beings are right in front of us during the meditation session. Then, we follow the same procedure as before, thinking that all of them have been our mothers in our past lives, and so forth. Sometimes we take all beings together as the object of meditation and generate the thought "May all beings be well and happy!" Sometimes we categorize beings based on their type of birth and cultivate altruistic love for the various kinds of beings separately. For example, "May all beings born in the hell of endless pain gain happiness and have the causes of happiness." At other times, we can categorize beings on the basis of the country or the place they live in. Sometimes, we can think of the beings living in Nepal, and at other times of those living in other countries. This is how we should train during our meditation sessions.

4. Training in post-meditation

When we meet others, as we walk outside during breaks for instance, we should generate the thought "May you be well and happy," or when we see a dog "May this dog be well and happy." This is how we should train ourselves. Whenever we see someone who is unwell or unhappy in any way, we should think "May you be well and happy," and when we see someone engaging in unwholesome deeds "May you engage in the causes of happiness." These two can be cultivated well separately. Also, sometimes we can reflect on the various types of wholesome deeds, which are the causes of happiness, and then generate the wish for beings who are deprived of these causes to attain them. By training ourselves in these various ways, our love will become multidimensional and very powerful.

We should do our best to make this loving concern for others very clear and stable in our mindstream in any given situation. When we meet people who do not know the Dharma, for instance, we can generate in ourselves the wish for them to study it. When we see people who are not generous, we can think "May they be able to give," and when we witness others behave recklessly, we can generate the sincere wish for them to maintain good discipline. There is a sūtra that explains thirty-two ways in which noble beings engage with others. When they encounter ignorant people, for example, they will think "It is no good that I develop wisdom while this person remains ignorant. May they too gain wisdom!" When they meet stingy people, they will think "I may practice generosity, but it is not good for this person to be stingy. May they too learn to give generously." These and thirty other attitudes of sublime beings are taught in this sūtra.

II. Cultivating Compassion

A. The Nature and the Benefits of Compassion

What is compassion? It is the wish for others, whoever it may be, to be free of suffering and not to engage in unwholesome actions, which are the causes of suffering. The causes of suffering are mental afflictions—i.e., self-grasping, desire and so forth—and the actions motivated by them.

Since compassion is especially important for those who want to train in the Mahāyāna, its benefits are clearly and extensively discussed in the sūtras. One sūtra states that if we wish to attain buddhahood, we do not need to practice many things; it is sufficient to cultivate compassion. All the qualities of a buddha will be ours if we have compassion. It is further taught that, as we first enter the path, it is compassion that will produce the

Mahāyāna bodhicitta in us, and once we are on the path, compassion will cause us to progress. When we eventually attain buddhahood, it is also compassion that will impel us to turn the Dharma wheel, and so forth, working for the benefit of countless beings and remaining with them for as long as space endures.

In one of his treatises, Nāgārjuna explains the specific benefits of the wholesome deeds that constitute the Mahāyāna path, stating that generosity is the cause for obtaining wealth and so forth. After this explanation, he says that all of these benefits are produced through compassion. In other words, compassion must precede all the practices of the Mahāyāna; it is what transforms all these deeds into the path. This is why the importance of compassion must be explained.

B. How to Cultivate Compassion

The method to cultivate compassion is straightforward. It is similar to the procedure followed in the practice of altruistic love and entails the following three progressive meditations: cultivating compassion toward those dear to us, toward those we do not like, and toward those for whom we have no particular feeling.

We begin, again, by thinking of our mother of this life, recollecting the kindness she has shown us, and developing the wish to repay her kindness, as explained earlier. Then follows the main meditation on compassion, which focuses on our mother's suffering and its causes, considering that our mother makes herself miserable, because she continues to commit many negative deeds, the result of which she will experience as suffering. For training during our formal meditation sessions, we visualize our mother in front of us and generate compassion in four different ways:

When we generate the thought "I wish for my mother to be free of suffering and not to engage in these negative deeds," it is called compassion associated with a wish. When we think "May my mother be free from suffering and the causes of suffering," it is compassion associated with aspiration. Sometimes we can think "May the Three Jewels think of my mother and help her be free from suffering and the causes of suffering," which is called compassion associated with prayer. The most important method here is the cultivation of compassion associated with what is called the extraordinary intention, or bodhicitta, by thinking "I will make it possible for my mother to be free from suffering and the causes of suffering." We train with these four methods to generate a genuine, pure compassion in our mind. We then apply the same methods to extend our compassion to others who are dear to us, to those who we do not like, and to those to whom we feel no particular connection.

Sometimes, we should cultivate compassion by focusing on specific types of beings subjected to great suffering. In the *Ornament of Mahāyāna Sūtras*, ten kinds of objects of compassion are listed, such as those who are excessively attached to sense pleasures; those who, even though they wish to practice the Dharma, are overpowered by obstacles; and so forth.[1] This treatise also mentions six other specific objects of compassion, namely those who are afflicted by factors directly opposed to the six perfections, such as strong miserliness, corrupted conduct, and so on.[2] Ārya Asaṅga speaks of 110 different objects of compassion in his teachings, and a sūtra speaks of sixteen types of compassion, such the compassion of those who teach the Dharma in order to tame the self-grasping of those afflicted by this wrong view.

In *Clarifying the Sage's Intent*, Sakya Paṇḍita explains that the bodhisattvas' compassion is directed toward two types of beings in particular: those who have entered the path of the Hīnayāna and worldly beings who continuously roam in saṃsāra. The latter are of two kinds: The first kind are those very powerful or wealthy people, or those who enjoy a privileged position in society, who not only continuously engage in negative actions themselves, but also cause others to commit them. Such beings are reborn in the lower realms as soon as they die, which is why they are considered special objects of compassion. The second kind are those who currently experience great sufferings. This includes the beings of the three lower realms, those in the higher realms who suffer terribly from severe diseases and the like, as well as those who carry the burden of having committed very serious misdeeds, breaking the law, and so forth.

Similarly, we should sometimes deeply contemplate how sentient beings live in general to instill the state of compassion:

> "Most beings engage in countless negative deeds, which are the causes for countless sufferings. I wish this was not so!"
>
> "All beings are controlled by their mental afflictions and dominated by their sufferings. This is so sad!"
>
> "Even though no one wants to suffer, they are subject to countless miseries and severe suffering and pain. How awful!"
>
> "Countless times they must endure the sufferings of the hot and cold hells! How horrible this is!"
>
> "Innumerable times they suffer from hunger and thirst in the realm of hungry ghosts! Oh my!"
>
> "In their countless rebirths in the animal realm, they suffer from being preyed upon and devoured by each other!"

"When they are born into the human world, they are oppressed by the sufferings of birth, old age, sickness, and death!"

"In each of their infinite lives as gods they suffer terribly from the signs of impending death and falling from their exalted state. These poor beings!"

"Entire oceans could be filled with the tears and the blood shed by a single being. If the flesh and bones of the lives of a single being were piled up, it would be greater than the largest mountain."

"Even for human beings like us, wherever we are born and wherever we live, there is no true happiness. It doesn't matter how strong or confident they are, all are controlled by mental afflictions and suffering. In this sense, all are miserable and wretched beings. This is truly sad! These afflictions are so difficult to overcome, and so beings roam endlessly in saṃsāra, life after life after life."

By familiarizing ourselves repeatedly with the mind of compassion through reflections like these, during both our formal sessions as well as during the phases of post-meditation, our compassion will become very powerful.

Avalokiteśvara said that the beings of the higher realms, like humans, commit negative deeds and accumulate the causes of suffering. The beings of the lower realms suffer the consequences of these deeds. Thinking about the plight of beings in this way, he gave rise to compassion for all beings in saṃsāra.

III. BODHICITTA

The next training related to the third line of the instructions on *Parting from the Four Attachments* is the cultivation of bodhicitta. It too entails three steps: cultivating bodhicitta in aspiration, cultivating the bodhicitta of equalizing oneself with others, and cultivating the bodhicitta of exchanging oneself for others. This is a very convenient way to structure the training in bodhicitta.

A. Aspiring Bodhicitta and Its Benefits

When we meditate on love and compassion, we generate the intention to lead all beings to happiness and to free them of suffering. Even though these are mere intentions, they yield great merit. However, we should not be satisfied with mere wishes, but seek a method to effectively help beings accomplish the happiness they desire and to free them from all the suffering they dread. What can we do to bring happiness to all beings and free them from suffering? Who can achieve such a task? Worldly leaders, powerful gods like Brahmā, and even highly realized arhats cannot accomplish this. They neither have the wish to achieve this, nor the ability. Only a fully awakened buddha has the ability to accomplish immeasurable benefit for others. For this reason, we generate the intention "I must attain buddhahood in order to lead all beings to happiness and to free them from suffering."

The aim is to accomplish the benefit of sentient beings, and the method to achieve this is bodhicitta, the mind of awakening. Based on this understanding, we generate the thought "I must attain the level of perfect awakening for the benefit of all sentient beings." This thought is called "aspiring bodhicitta."

Without this resolve, it is impossible to attain the perfect awakening of buddhahood. Regardless of how great the good actions we have gathered may be, they cannot become the cause for complete enlightenment without bodhicitta. In other words, the resultant state of buddhahood depends on the Mahāyāna resolve for awakening, that is, bodhicitta. The teachings therefore extol its many great benefits. It is said, for example, that those who properly give rise to bodhicitta become bodhisattvas, which means that they become worthy of offerings and praise from the entire world, including the gods. Bodhicitta has these and many other inconceivable virtues.

We must bear in mind, however, that genuine altruistic love, compassion, and bodhicitta do not arise easily in our mindstream. It takes months and years of dedicated practice. It is therefore important to accumulate many, many moments of wholesome mental states that are beneficial both in the short term and in the long run to oneself and others. We can do this by using our mālā to count the number of repetitions. If we do this with undistracted attention, the benefits will be great.

> "May all beings enjoy happiness and have the causes of happiness!"
> "May all beings be free of suffering and the causes of suffering!"
> "I must attain the perfect awakening of a buddha in order to benefit all sentient beings!"

Reciting these aspirations over and over again, even a few hundred-thousand times, will certainly have a very beneficial impact on the mind. Apart from that, we should also keep praying to the Three Jewels for the meaning of these lines to be born in our mindstream and engage in the various practices to gather the accumulations and purify our obscurations. All these methods are very important.

If we do not understand the teachings we receive or doubt their truthfulness, or if we think that we cannot or, indeed, do not need to practice, this indicates that the latencies of goodness present in our mindstream are still dormant. In other words, we have not been able to bring to maturation the karmic seeds of the good deeds accumulated in our past lives. Therefore, to awaken or mature these wholesome seeds, it is important that we pray, accumulate wholesome actions, and purify obscurations. This will help us understand the Dharma well and practice in accordance with our understanding.

In brief, anyone who has entered the Mahāyāna path—whether they are lay practitioners or ordained—requires renunciation, love, compassion, and bodhicitta. There is no Mahāyāna Dharma if we lack these elements. But if we have managed to generate them well in our mind, we will have no regrets at the time of our death.

B. The Bodhicitta Vow and the Training

There are no formal vows of love and compassion, but there is the vow of bodhicitta. Why is it important for Mahāyāna practitioners to take the bodhicitta vow? Generally speaking, there are two types of wholesome deeds: those that are conjoined with vows and those that are not. The latter, also called middling wholesome deeds, refers to any wholesome action accomplished by someone who does not hold a vow related to that action. Such actions are not wasted, they will produce good results, but they cannot help us attain liberation or buddhahood. For us to progress on the path, it is therefore important to first take a vow and then unfailingly follow the training of abandoning the unwholesome deeds related to that particular vow so as not to impair it. We must then also gradually train ourselves in accomplishing whatever wholesome deeds we can, according to our capacity. This is the training in accomplishing wholesome deeds. Observing these two precepts will genuinely improve our practice.

There are two traditions for the ritual of imparting the bodhicitta vow: the Cittamātra tradition and the Madhyamaka tradition. Of these two, the vow according to Cittamātra is more difficult to bestow and to maintain. First, the recipient must already hold Buddhist vows, either those of a lay person or of an ordained Sangha member. It is therefore more difficult to initially obtain it. In terms of the number of vows to be observed, there are four major and forty-six minor transgressions according to the Cittamātra tradition. Regardless of the individual capacities of the recipients, whether they are of superior or inferior acumen, if one has received the bodhicitta vow in this tradition, all these vows must be kept together. In other words, in this tradition there is no gradual training in the precepts.

The training in the precepts of the bodhicitta vow according to the Madhyamaka tradition ultimately also consists of abandoning all faults and accomplishing all virtues and perfections. However, this tradition allows for a gradual training in the meantime. When we first take the vow, we say the words: "I will gradually train." This means that we promise to progressively accomplish wholesome deeds and abandon misdeeds to the extent possible according to our capacity. Therefore, it is permissible to train in a gradual manner once we have obtained the vow of bodhicitta with these words. The reason for this is that practitioners of the Mahāyāna are grouped into three categories—inferior, middling, and superior—based on their mental tendencies and capacities, and the way these individuals train varies accordingly. For these reasons, the bodhicitta vow according to the Madhyamaka tradition is more convenient to receive and easier to maintain, and its benefits are indeed great.

1. The training for individuals of lesser capacity

For individuals of lesser capacity, the training in aspiring bodhicitta simply consists in maintaining the wish to attain buddhahood in order to benefit all beings and to guard it from declining. In terms of their training in engaging bodhicitta, they can abandon as many unwholesome deeds as is possible for them. If, due to their own ignorance, out of negligence, or under the influence of other afflictions, they commit transgressions or engage in unwholesome deeds that go against their precepts, these should be properly confessed. Their training in engaging bodhicitta in terms of wholesome deeds consists in accomplishing as many good deeds as they can, dedicating the merits of these actions, and rejoicing the past and present good actions performed by themselves and others. Buddha himself declared that those who are engaged in many activities, such as lay practitioners, can follow the path in this way.

It is very important for us to overcome our faintheartedness and our lack of confidence. "How could I, a lowly, wretched being, possibly ever attain the state of perfection called buddhahood, endowed with immeasurable qualities?" If we think like that, we allow ourselves to give in to faintheartedness. This attitude is a serious obstacle as it will prevent us from bringing forth the effort needed to follow the path. If, due to such lack of confidence, we do not strive in our practice, we will never be able to overcome our present condition. It is therefore important for us to take heart and generate confidence. "The protector Maitreya stated that in every single moment many beings attain perfect awakening. Why should we, therefore, not be able to accomplish it?" This is how we should think to encourage ourselves and generate confidence.

Ārya Nāgārjuna similarly explained that the buddhas of the past neither fell from the sky like rain, nor did they emerge from the ground like crops. Like us, they first generated the resolve to attain supreme awakening and then practiced with great diligence. In other words, they became buddhas through their training on the path. In the *Way of the Bodhisattva*, the great master Śāntideva says that the Buddha himself declared that even insects could become buddhas if they put forth the necessary effort. Compared to them it is relatively easy for a human to attain complete awakening.

2. The training for individuals of middling capacity

For individuals of middling capacity, the training consists of abandoning the so-called four dark dharmas and pursuing the four bright dharmas. The four dark dharmas are four types of negative deeds that, if not abandoned, will prevent us from obtaining bodhicitta again in our next life. Hence, the importance of knowing them. They are:

(1) To intentionally lie to a holy being in order to deceive them

(2) To disparage a bodhisattva or speak about their faults

(3) To cause regret in those who engage in wholesome deeds by telling them that what they are doing is not right

(4) To harm others through deceit

The four white dharmas are:

(1) Not lying

(2) Placing others on the Mahāyāna path

(3) Praising the bodhisattvas

(4) Maintaining a genuine altruistic attitude toward others

Furthermore, there are four transgressions of our precepts, which include not teaching the Dharma and not practicing generosity with one's possessions due to stinginess and attachment, and so forth.[3] These are actions we must abstain from.

3. The training for individuals of highest capacity

The extensive training in aspiring bodhicitta for individuals of highest capacity involves cultivating love and compassion, serving a spiritual teacher, generating faith in the Three Jewels, and so forth. Furthermore, since māras or evil forces will create obstacles for those who have generated the resolve of bodhicitta, the training also entails knowing how to identify and deal with such obstacles. This includes supplicating the buddhas and bodhisattvas to avert the activities of the māras.[4]

The seven-limb practice is said to be especially important for extensive training in engaging bodhicitta. For this reason, we are instructed to perform the seven-limb practice three times a day and three times a night in the presence of the buddhas and bodhisattvas.

C. The Bodhicitta Practice of Equalizing Oneself with Others

The bodhicitta practice of equalizing oneself with others is very straightforward. Just as we want to be happy ourselves, all other beings long for happiness as well, and just as we do not want to suffer, others equally dread suffering. It is easy to understand that we are all exactly the same in this regard. When people fail to acknowledge this fact, however, they cannot agree with each other. But once we appreciate this fact, we can generate the wish "I must accomplish the happiness and well-being of both myself and others, and overcome my own and others' suffering." This is the attitude of equalizing oneself with others.

Next is the practice of exchanging oneself for others. To exchange oneself for others fundamentally means to offer one's happiness and the positive potential of one's own wholesome deeds to others, and to take upon oneself their suffering and the negative potential of their unwholesome deeds.

This practice is mainly carried out at first on the mental level and then should also be applied in daily life. Some Tibetan masters argued that it is not really possible to exchange positive and negative deeds and happiness and suffering in this way. According to them, to "exchange oneself with others" actually means to exchange cherishing oneself for cherishing others. It means to forsake the attitude of self-cherishing, which has been with us since time without beginning, and to cherish others instead. However, the glorious protector Ārya Nāgārjuna clearly stated that we must exchange our wholesome deeds for the misdeeds of others, and the bodhisattva Śāntideva repeatedly taught the same as well.

In short, we must exchange everything. For this, we must make it a habit to accept everything undesirable and of poor quality, and to offer to others all the good and desirable things we may have. If we own some nice clothes, for instance, we can offer them to someone in need and exchange them for their poor clothes. When we have some good food, we can give it to someone else and eat their inferior meal instead. This also constitutes the practice of exchanging happiness for suffering. In *The Way of the Bodhisattva*, Śāntideva similarly mentions many other ways to put this practice of exchange into action. When we find ourselves in a privileged or higher position, for instance, we can exchange it with someone less fortunate.

Usually, we try to hide our faults and secretly wish for others to have their misdeeds exposed. Sometimes we even blame others for the faults we ourselves have committed. Conversely, bodhisattvas are very transparent and openly reveal to others their own mistakes; they also take personal responsibility for the misdeeds committed by others. These are ways of applying the practice of exchanging oneself for others in daily life.

Due to our attitude of self-cherishing, we usually seek fame and recognition and do not want others, particularly our enemies, to enjoy the same. When we practice exchanging ourselves for others, however, we should strive to praise others in a way that completely outshines our own name and reputation.

Similarly, due to our self-cherishing, we look around to see if others might have things that could be of use to us, and if we find no other means to acquire them, we might even think of stealing them. To practice exchanging oneself for others, we reverse this kind of thinking and instead see if we own things that could be of benefit to others. And even if we are not yet able to give away our possessions, we should practice it at least in thought, imagining that we are stealing these things from ourselves to give them to others.

What are the faults of not engaging in the practice of exchanging oneself for others? First of all, it is taught that we simply will not be able to achieve buddhahood, and even in this life, we will not be truly happy. People who only think of themselves and who are not concerned about others—some are not even concerned about the well-being of their own parents and relatives—perceive everyone as a threat. Such people spend their lives without the support of others. They consequently face many difficulties in their lives and might even end up abandoned and alone.

Most people are only concerned that things are going well for themselves. They want to win, be famous, and so forth. But we should reflect on how this kind of self-cherishing attitude is actually the cause of all kinds of conflict. It is due to this mindset that parents argue with their children, leaders with their employees and followers, teachers with their students, and life partners with each other. The antidote for all these conflicts is the cultivation of bodhicitta.

The rationale behind this practice is the following. To merely abandon self-grasping is not that extraordinary, since śrāvaka arhats have also achieved that much. Beyond that, we need to develop the attitude of being deeply concerned with the welfare of others. This practice of benefiting others is the way of the Mahāyāna.

The formal practice of exchanging oneself for others follows the same pattern as the practice of loving kindness. Beginning with our own mother, the objects of our practice are grouped into three categories. First, we visualize in front of us the being we are focusing on—our mother for instance—and then generate the wish "May all the suffering and the all afflictions, the causes of sufferings, that torment her as well as all other beings, and all the misfortunes and flaws that make this world so miserable be transferred to me, and through this, may all beings become free of afflictions and suffering."

D. Tonglen, the Practice of Exchanging Oneself for Others

1. The nature and practice of tonglen

The practice of exchanging oneself for others is carried out by means of two activities: giving (Tib. "*tong*") and taking ("*len*"). In this practice, in terms of *taking*, there are two types of beings from whom we do not take anything upon ourselves. The first of these are the buddhas, since there is nothing unwanted in them for us to take upon ourselves, and the second are our gurus, as they are the objects of our devotion. Excepting them, we take upon ourselves all flaws of all sentient beings, including those of the bodhisattvas on the tenth bhūmi.

In terms of *giving*, it is alright to practice giving towards all beings, including the buddhas. To practice giving, we think that we give completely all our merit, well-being, and happiness to all beings and we also offer them to the buddhas. We do this with the intention that all our good deeds and all our happiness is given completely to each and every being individually. We should then think that through this giving, all these beings are blessed on a temporary level with good health and mental well-being, and that they enjoy prosperity and success in their endeavor. They also obtain all the inner conditions needed for the attainment of buddhahood, such as compassion and faith, as well as all the necessary outer conditions, including having a teacher, Dharma friends, material support, and so forth. In this way, they immediately come closer to the attainment of complete awakening.

To practice *taking*, we can sometimes visualize the misdeeds and sufferings of all beings in the form of dark smoke that is absorbed into our heart and think "May everything that beings do not want ripen upon me!" For *giving*, we visualize white light issuing from our heart towards all beings and think "May all beings have happiness and the causes of happiness."

We can also combine this practice with the recitation of verses from the teachings of the great masters. When we practice *taking*, we can recite, for example, this verse from Nāgārjuna, "May the suffering of all beings, my mothers, ripen upon me!" and repeat this line many times. We can use our mālā to count one hundred recitations of this verse, while thinking that all these things come to us. For *giving*, we recite "May my goodness and well-being bring my mothers' true happiness!" and think that they all attain genuine well-being by giving them all your good deeds and well-being. This too should be repeated over and over again. In fact, we should accumulate many hundred thousand repetitions of these and similar recitations. This form of practice can be very efficient and really transform our mind.

This crucial point is made in the third chapter of *The Way of the Bodhisattva*, where it is stated:

> My body and likewise my possessions,
> And all the goodness gained throughout the threefold time (etc.).[5]

This verse expresses the wish to be able to relinquish completely all the bodies and possessions we have had until now, as well as all our roots of goodness, to every single sentient being. This is the promise we make when we say, "I give them all away."

How should we think to actualize this commitment? This is shown in lines such as "May I be a protector for those who need protection, a bridge for those who wish to cross a river, a dwelling for those in need of shelter, a lamp for those who need a light, a priceless jewel for the destitute and poor; may I be for them like a wish-fulfilling tree" and so forth. We should deliberately familiarize ourselves with thoughts like "By being a wish-fulfilling tree or a precious jewel, I can greatly benefit others." When we genuinely engage in the bodhisattva path, as expressed in *The Way of the Bodhisattva*, we generate the aspiration to be like the four great elements of earth, water, fire, and air, which benefit beings in so many ways, and like empty space that provides the room needed to move and function in the world. Thus, we make the aspiration that our bodies, our wealth, and the roots of goodness accumulated throughout the three times may similarly benefit beings in numerous ways until they attain buddhahood.

We can use any situation to train our minds. When we eat good food, we can make the aspiration "May all beings obtain the root of goodness that allows them to enjoy good food like this." When we have bad food, we can similarly make the wish "May the bad karma of all beings who have to eat bad food ripen upon me." Everything can be utilized in this way. Simply put in terms of good and bad, we generate the thought "May all bad things come to me and may all good things come to others!"

Master Serlingpa taught that we should think as follows:

> When you experience hardship or pain, pray "May the difficulties of all beings ripen upon me! May it cause the ocean of suffering to dry up!"
>
> When you experience happiness, pray "May all beings experience happiness like this! May all of space be filled with well-being, happiness, and joy!"

2. On the benefits of exchanging oneself for others

It is said that the recitation of the words "May the suffering of my mother-sentient beings ripen upon me!" together with a single brief instant of meditation on its meaning generates immeasurable merit. In *The Way of the Bodhisattva*, as well as in *An Analysis of the Three Vows*,[6] it is taught that the bodhicitta practice of exchanging oneself for others is the fastest path to buddhahood. It is also called the "secret path," because it is so difficult for individuals who lack merit to trust in this practice. It is also said to be the essence of the Buddha's teaching. In brief, the practice of exchanging oneself for others is the highest of all the paths to liberation taught in the sūtras.

The Lord of Dharma Sakya Paṇḍita explained that, as a support for our practice of bodhicitta, it is important for us to understand why it is harmful to work for one's own benefit and why it is beneficial to accomplish the benefit of others. In other words, why is it so important for us to generate the Mahāyāna bodhicitta? This has many reasons. First of all, the object we are focusing on with the thought of bodhicitta are all sentient beings. At some point of our existence in saṃsāra, every sentient being has been our own mother. They have therefore benefited us greatly in the past. In terms of the path, we rely on other beings to generate loving kindness, compassion, and bodhicitta, and to practice the six perfections and the four means to gather beings. To attain buddhahood, we must bring joy to others and gladden their hearts. It is not possible to attain complete awakening without accomplishing the benefit of beings.

There are two objects based on which we can accumulate merit: sentient beings and buddhas. Based on the buddhas we generate merit by developing faith, offering prostrations, and so forth. This is why the buddhas are like a field for us where we can harvest merit. Based on sentient beings we can develop loving kindness, compassion, and bodhicitta, and practice the six perfections of generosity, ethical discipline, and so on, and the four means of gathering. In this sense, they too are a field of merit. Sentient beings in saṃsāra are deprived of true happiness and have no choice but to suffer. Based on the fact that they lack the happiness they seek and endure the suffering they fear, we generate loving kindness, compassion, and bodhicitta. When we familiarize ourselves with these thoughts and cultivate them, our path becomes excellent indeed.

In *The Way of the Bodhisattva*, Śāntideva compares the faults of being selfish to the benefits of accomplishing the welfare of others.[7] He says, for instance, that when ordinary people seek to gain a higher position to stand out among their peers, they are instead reborn in the lower realms, and even should they attain a birth in the higher realms, they find themselves in miserable conditions. Conversely, bodhisattvas have the humblest ambitions, aspiring, for example, to be nothing more than janitors or street sweepers. As a result, they always take the lowest position, thinking that there is no one inferior to them: "Below me, I only find water and the bridges and roads I walk on." This is how we should think. If we manage to do this, we will naturally possess the wish to help others accomplish sublime goals, rather than pursue them for ourselves. As a result, Śāntideva says, we will be reborn in the higher realms, where we will enjoy many advantages and benefits.

He further states that if we harm others with the intention to derive benefit from it, we will experience the suffering of the hell realms and other terrible conditions. However, if we voluntarily undergo harm in order to benefit others, we will experience the fortunes of a good rebirth. When we make others our servants, we will, as a result, spend many lives involuntarily serving others. However, if we readily serve others, we can become great leaders in the future.

"How can we make the mind wholesome?" In response to this question, it is explained in a sūtra that we can accomplish this by repeatedly cultivating the attitude of appreciating others and treating them with great respect, and assuming the humblest or most inferior position. When our teacher the Buddha was a bodhisattva on the path, he thought of himself as the lowest among all his companions; he physically prostrated to them and praised them with his speech. As a result of these actions, not only sentient beings venerated him once he became a buddha, but even the flowers and trees respectfully bowed to him.

Similarly, if we are arrogant and denigrate others, saying that they do not understand the Dharma, that they are utterly incapable or stupid, we will end up dull-witted in our future lives. This is called the result concordant with the cause. If we take pride in our looks and look down on others due to their appearance, we will have unattractive physical features in our future lives. Again, if we belittle others, seeing them as mere servants or as wretched beings who merely consume other people's food, while taking pride in our own wealth and social standing, we will experience a miserable future existence. These are just some of the examples given to illustrate the faults of self-cherishing and the benefits of cherishing others. "In brief," Śāntideva emphasizes, "the buddhas have attained complete awakening as a result of working for the benefit of others and ordinary beings are still roaming in saṃsāra because they only strive to accomplish their own good."[8]

E. The Six Perfections

1. The nature of the perfections

The essence of the Mahāyāna path consists of the six perfections, or pāramitās. I will therefore explain them briefly here. The Tibetan term for pāramitā is *pa-röl-tu chin-pa*.[9] *Pa röl* means "farther shore" and indicates the state that is beyond both saṃsāra and nirvāṇa, in order words, the level of complete awakening or buddhahood. The methods to achieve this realization are therefore labeled "gone to the farther shore."[10] All six perfections are in fact mental states differentiated based on their different activities.

2. The perfection of generosity

a. The nature of generosity

The first of the six perfections is generosity. Generosity is the name given to the thought of wanting to give to others whatever one has in order to benefit them. The opposing factor to generosity is stinginess, the cause of which is attachment to possessions. Stinginess can cause one to commit very negative actions and brings about great misfortune. It is the cause for rebirth as a hungry ghost, and even if one is born in the higher realms, one will be poor as a result of it. Having attachment to possessions is therefore a great mistake; it will rob one of the opportunity to practice the Dharma, and this, in turn, will prevent one from attaining liberation.

Generally, two types of generosity are distinguished: pure generosity and impure generosity. Impure generosity would be, for example, giving others alcohol, meat, or poison, or to offer members of the monastic community food after noon. In terms of pure generosity, we can again differentiate various kinds, such as generosity that leads to rebirth in the higher realms, generosity through which one attains the result of the śrāvaka path, and so forth. Among the various kinds of generosity, the perfection of generosity is the generosity that leads to the attainment of buddhahood. This is the type of generosity we are discussing here.

For generosity to be a perfection, it must be complete, having the right preparation, the right accomplishment, and the right conclusion. This structure equally applies to the other perfections as well. The preparation is the motivation of bodhicitta: "In order to benefit all beings, I must attain buddhahood. For that purpose, I will engage in this activity." This motivation must be present, regardless of how great or small our act of giving, etc. might be. Then, while we engage in the actual deed, we relate to it with the correct view, knowing that the action itself is emptiness. This is the right accomplishment. Finally, as a conclusion, we dedicate the merit of our action, forming the intention that it may be a cause for us to attain buddhahood for the benefit of all beings. When we practice the pāramitās in this way, complete with the three aspects of preparation, accomplishment, and conclusion, they become an integral part of the Mahāyāna path.

b. Three forms of generosity and the right preparation

Coming back to the practice of generosity, the teachings speak of three types of giving: giving material goods, giving fearlessness, and giving the Dharma.[11] For the generosity of giving the Dharma, the teacher should be motivated by compassion, thinking that they will explain the Dharma to help others be free of ignorance and other afflictions. When the Dharma is taught in a faultless manner and based on this motivation, it is the generosity of giving the Dharma. This also means that we must be wary of hidden agendas. It is important that one does not teach with the intention to gain anything from it, whether it is material wealth, respect, the reputation of being very learned, or gratitude from the listeners. All these intentions are expressions of the attachment to gain and to honor. When someone teaches Dharma with this motivation, it is not true Dharma they practice. As it was stated by Mañjuśrī: "If you are attached to this life, you are not a Dharma practitioner." The instructions on *Parting from the Four Attachments* are extremely beneficial for our Dharma activities and our practice. Students of the Mahāyāna should really examine themselves through the lens of these four lines to check whether the way they engage with the Dharma is free from these four attachments.

The generosity of giving material goods consists of giving away both outer wealth, our possessions, and inner wealth, our body. Due to our strong habituation to stinginess, rooted in our attachment to these things, even thinking of giving them away is very difficult, let alone actually doing it. However, this kind of generosity is indeed an excellent practice. It is therefore important that we train ourselves in it. First, we should try to cultivate appreciation for generosity by repeatedly thinking how important it is to learn to give. When we see a beggar, for instance, we might perceive them as someone who will harm or annoy us. Instead of letting ourselves be overcome by such thoughts, we should think, "This is not someone who will harm me. On the contrary, this person will benefit me greatly. He will help me accumulate merit and swiftly attain enlightenment." Then, such encounters will bring us great joy, instead of troubling our minds. For us to generate this attitude, it is important to learn about the benefits of generosity and the harmful effects of stinginess from the sūtras and śāstras, and to think about them repeatedly on a regular basis.

It is taught that monks and nuns should not practice generosity by giving material goods. This form of the practice is therefore not their concern. This is because members of the monastic community are not supposed to concern themselves with gathering and managing material wealth. Their main responsibility is to maintain their ethical discipline and to engage in the activities of hearing, reflecting, and meditation. If they occupied themselves with giving material goods, it would become an obstacle for their studies and meditation. They should, however, practice the generosity of giving the Dharma.

To increase our ability to give generously we should frequently contemplate the Buddha's words on it. He stated, for instance, that ordinary people admire those who hoard their wealth, but the buddhas praise those who give it to others. The very act of gathering possessions and keeping them for oneself is a cause for remaining in saṃsāra; while the act of giving them away is a cause for attaining buddhahood. Moreover, there is absolutely no certainty that whatever we gathered will be ours alone. It may very well become wealth that we will share with others, including thieves. We may have accumulated it by ourselves, but we won't be alone to spend it. If we freely give it to others, however, the merit born from our generosity cannot be stolen; it will be ours. These and many other reflections on generosity are found in the sūtras.

The third type of generosity is giving fearlessness. It means, for example, to protect someone from punishment by a ruling authority or from being harmed by the elements of fire, water, and so forth, as well as protecting others from rebirth in the lower realms.

c. The actual act of giving

When we train ourselves in the actual act of giving, we should begin by giving things of little value and gradually increase the scope of our generosity. If we rush into it and immediately perform great acts of generosity, we might come to regret them later and abandon the practice. To avoid this, we begin small, with a glass of water, something to eat, or a very small amount of money. Then, we train by gradually increasing the scope of our giving until, one day, we are able to give everything we have.

In the same way, we should also widen the range of recipients. At first, we might give to those connected to us in the Dharma, such as our master, other teachers, and the monastic community. If we are unable in the current moment to give to ordinary beings and to those in need, it is good to train ourselves in this way and then gradually give to others as well, until we can freely give to everyone.

In terms of the frequency of giving, we can begin by practicing generosity on auspicious days and then extend our practice to ordinary days as well. We can train ourselves by choosing any day and deciding to make it a day of generosity until, eventually, we practice it all the time. The most important thing is that we actually start giving. Generosity is the first of the six causes of buddhahood. If we don't cultivate it now, even if we attain a human rebirth, we will be poor. Poverty can cause so much misery and it can be a great obstacle for Dharma practice. This is why we really must practice generosity, beginning now.

When we give to a beggar, for instance, it is important that we don't relate to them with contempt and abuse or reprimand them. This would be wrong. We should sincerely rejoice in the opportunity and be friendly and respectful. If we offer them whatever we intend to give in this way, it will be a very beneficial act. If we have the time, we should give to others personally with our own two hands; this is also very positive. Moreover, if we have something we can give now, we should not postpone our giving but do it straight away; and if we have the choice, we should not select an item of inferior quality to give to others but give the best we have.

d. How to correctly accomplish the perfection of generosity

The protector Maitreya taught that whenever we practice any of the six perfections, our action must possess four features to become a perfection. When we practice generosity, for example, regardless of what kind of giving we are engaged in, it should (1) act as an antidote to the opposing factor of generosity, that is stinginess; (2) be embraced by the wisdom that knows the emptiness of the act of giving; (3) have the ability to fulfill the needs of others; and (4) gladden the minds of the recipients to gradually lead them to the path of whichever vehicle is most suitable to them.

Moreover, our practice should be free of the faults of seven attachments. In the case of generosity, these are: (1) attachment to our possessions; (2) attachment to procrastination, thinking that we will give later; (3) being satisfied by giving just a little; (4) hoping to receive something in return for our giving in this life; and (5) hoping for a good karmic result in future lives. These two expectations are particularly problematic. It is said that if we give to others with the hope for a return or for karmic fruits, our practice becomes a business. This is not the path of the bodhisattvas. When we give something to others, we should therefore think that, along with whatever it is we are giving, we also offer them the result of the root of goodness generated through our generosity. (6) Our giving should also be free of attachment to its opposing factor, that is, not wanting to rid ourselves of stinginess, and (7) to "distractions." The last one includes two forms of "distraction," namely the wish to attain the resultant state of the śrāvaka path and thinking that the three spheres of the action of giving[12] are truly existent, instead of seeing them as illusory.

It is also important to train by integrating all the perfections into the practice of each single one. In fact, not doing so would incur many mistakes. When we are giving something away, for example, the act of giving itself constitutes generosity. Not wishing to attain the state of a śrāvaka arhat as a result of one's giving and harboring no attachment to benefits experienced in this life constitute ethical discipline. Forbearance can be the act of not getting angry when insulted or abused by the person one is giving to. To be pleased by the giving is diligence; dedicating it by making the wish that this act of generosity may be a cause for attaining buddhahood is meditative concentration; and knowing that generosity is emptiness is wisdom. In this way, all perfections are included in the single practice of generosity, and the same principle applies to each of the other perfections.

3. The beneficial results of the perfections

The benefits common to all the perfections are explained in a very convenient way in a sūtra, where it is stated that: they (1) defeat their opposing factors, such as stinginess and so forth; (2) are the causes for attaining buddhahood; (3) are very beneficial for both oneself and others in this life; (4) and will produce excellent results in our next and futures lives. I would like to encourage everyone to keep these benefits in mind.

The Fourth Line: "If There Is Grasping, It Is Not the View."

Introduction

I would like to remind you to receive these teachings neither out of attachment to this life, nor out of attachment to saṃsāra, but to think that you are studying the Dharma to attain buddhahood for the benefit of all beings.

The Jonang master Kunga Drolchok collected the pith instructions of many Tibetan lineages and compiled them into what is known as the *Hundred Instructions from Jonang*.[1] These include teachings from all four major schools of Tibetan Buddhism prevalent today. Kunga Drolchok felt that the teachings on *Parting from the Four Attachments* were the most beneficial for him to turn his mind to the Dharma. To acknowledge this, he placed these teachings at the very beginning of the collection.

For the time being, we will leave the next three perfections—ethical discipline, forbearance, and diligence—to focus on the perfections of meditation and wisdom, or calm abiding and profound insight,[2] since these topics require more explanation.

I. The Perfection of Meditation

A. Why Meditate?

Why do we practice meditation? Or in other words, what are the unwanted consequences of not training in calm abiding and states of meditative concentration? For one, our mind will be easily distracted, which in turn opens the door to all other mental afflictions. Actions, including the recitation of sacred texts, will not be of great benefit to us if we perform them with a distracted mind. The Lamdré master Sönam Tenpa stated that activities of body and speech carried out with a mind that is distracted towards the three times are meaningless since they bring no benefit whatsoever.

Second, without the stability of concentration it is impossible to effectively apply the view. To understand the view, we study the teachings on Madhyamaka, the philosophy of the Middle Way. This is very important because we should first have a correct understanding of the view before familiarizing ourselves with it through the practice of profound insight. In other words, there is no practice of profound insight without the right view and the mind of calm abiding. If the mind cannot be focused unwaveringly on the view, there can be no direct realization of the true nature of reality. Lacking this realization, it is impossible to uproot the afflictions and thus to overcome suffering. These are the unwanted consequences for us.

Furthermore, if we do not attain states of meditative concentration through the practice of calm abiding, we will not gain the supernatural abilities.[3] This, in turn, will make it very difficult for us to genuinely benefit others. However, if we do practice meditation, we can accomplish the path of calm abiding and profound insight, through which we will be able to attain whatever we aspire to without great difficulties, including liberation from saṃsāra and the omniscient state of buddhahood.

What is the nature of meditative concentration? It is a mind that remains continuously focused on a wholesome object for an extended period. Three types of meditative concentration are distinguished. The first are called "meditative concentrations of pleasant abodes experienced in this life."[4] These concentrations possess the happiness of being free of attachment to the body and the mind, and they directly affect one's well-being in this life. This is why they are called "pleasant abodes experienced in this life." The second are "meditative concentrations that accomplish excellent qualities." These are the immeasurable common and uncommon samādhis cultivated by bodhisattvas. They are given that name because they are the basis for these bodhisattvas to attain manifold excellent qualities. The third are called "meditative concentrations that accomplish the benefit of others." Through the power of these concentrations, bodhisattvas are able to do whatever is necessary to help others, such as curing diseases, extending lifespan, bestowing wealth, and so forth.

B. The Prerequisites for Samādhi

To cultivate meditative absorption, or samādhi, we must first assemble the necessary conditions. Jowo Je Palden Atiśa stated that, if the conditions do not come together, we simply will not attain calm abiding, even if we were to meditate for a thousand years.

Kamalaśīla and Asaṅga both speak of six necessary conditions. The first is the place. We need a good environment appropriate for the cultivation of samādhi. It should be a place (1) where whatever is needed for the practice is easy to find; (2) that is located in a safe environment, meaning, there is no danger of harm from venomous snakes or other creatures; (3) that is not exposed to extreme natural conditions, such as flooding and so forth; and (4) that is quiet, meaning not visited by people during the day and silent at night. Most importantly, it should be a place (5) where we can live with good Dharma friends. These are people whose view and conduct are in harmony with ours, who possess excellent qualities, are well-educated in the Dharma, practice meditation, and have experience. We should seek the company of such excellent companions or, if possible, that of our teacher. In such an environment our own qualities and our understanding of the Dharma will naturally develop.

The second condition is to have few needs: we should not seek anything better or greater than our current conditions. The third is contentment, which means that we are satisfied with what we have. The fourth is to abstain from worldly activities. This means that we should not think about our finances, including the accounts of our monastery, we should not listen to the news, and so forth. Putting aside all activities and causes of distraction, we should be deaf and blind to the world.

The fifth and most important condition is to observe pure ethical discipline, meaning that we carefully guard whatever vows we have taken. In fact, ethical discipline is the uncommon condition for samādhi. Among the six perfections, the respectively previous ones are the causes for the respectively later ones. That is to say, the first four perfections serve as the foundation for meditative absorption. Likewise, among the three higher trainings, discipline, the first, is the condition for samādhi, the second, which in turn is the condition for wisdom.

The sixth condition is discussed extensively by Śāntideva in the chapter on meditation concentration in his *The Way of the Bodhisattva*. He explains that to cultivate the meditative states, we need to "leave behind the world and relinquish discursive thought." Here, the "world" signifies our attachment to beings, in particular to our friends, relatives, and anyone we hold dear, as well as to material possessions. "Discursive thought" refers to any uncontrolled thinking other than these two. To stay in isolation but failing to relinquish these thoughts is like staying in a frozen house: it will only bring problems. We should therefore strive to overcome them.

It is generally advised to prepare well for the periods of meditation. In the time leading up to intensive meditation practice, we should refrain from doing much physical work, we should speak little and reduce our recitation practices, and our mind should also not be stimulated by thinking about various projects and so forth. Furthermore, we should also set aside a significant period of time to devote ourselves to the practice.[5]

C. The Actual Practice of Meditation

1. Preliminary reflections and prayers

For the practice of meditation itself, we should stay in a suitable place, prepare a comfortable meditation seat facing an altar, and arrange offerings in front of it. Then, to begin the actual session, we recall the four lines of the instructions on *Parting from the Four Attachments*. The foundation for our entire practice is laid through the contemplations of death and impermanence, of the freedoms and favorable conditions that are so difficult to assemble, and so forth, followed by the generation of loving kindness, compassion, etc. We should deeply reflect on these subjects and recite the relevant lines and prayers to bring up the right motivation for the practice. We should, in fact, keep these reflections with us at all times, not only for the beginning of a session but throughout our day. This will certainly affect our mind in a very beneficial way.

After these initial reflections, we take refuge and recite the supplication prayers, generate bodhicitta, and perform the practice in seven branches.[6] Among the supplications related to the instructions on *Parting from the Four Attachments*, we should focus on the line: "Grant your blessings so that deluded perceptions may subside into the ultimate expanse." Recite this special prayer many times as it directly relates to the practice of calm abiding and profound insight indicated by the words: "If there is grasping, it is not the view."

2. The object of meditation

To cultivate the mind of calm abiding, we require an object to focus on. Several different objects are mentioned in the teachings. Suitable outer objects include a buddha image, or earth, water, and so on for meditation on the bases of totality.[7] Inner objects include meditation on the body as a skeleton, mindfulness of the breath, and so forth. Among all these objects it is generally advised to use a buddha image as a focal support for meditation. The reason being that focusing on the form of a buddha will have many benefits besides developing concentration, such as generating trust and devotion. We can use a painted image or a statue as practice support. In the Lamdré tradition the drawing of a blue flower is used as focal support for meditation. The flower should be about three inches wide. The color blue is used because it is soothing for the eyes. Alternatively, one can also use a blue piece of cloth.

The focal support is placed about an arm's length in front of oneself, at a suitable height so that our sustained gaze does not cause discomfort. It is also important that the object is completely still. Some teachers argue that one should not look at external forms in meditation. However, there are reasons why doing so is actually very beneficial.

3. The posture

Regarding the meditation posture, we should sit on a comfortable seat and adopt an appropriate posture. If possible, we sit in the vajra posture with fully crossed legs, like the posture of Vairocana. Otherwise, we can also sit in the so-called sattva posture, which resembles a half-vajra posture, with one leg drawn in, like the posture of Āryā Tārā. It is important that we sit upright with a straight back, leaning neither to the right nor to the left, neither forward nor backward. Our head should also be held in balance, neither raised, nor lowered, and our shoulders are held level.

Our eyes should be neither wide open, which would give rise to mental agitation, nor closed, which would induce drowsiness. Instead, our eyes should be half-closed, the lids covering about half of the eyeballs, with our gaze directed towards the tip of our nose. Our jaw is relaxed, and our lips are left neutral so that our mouth is not shut tight, and our tongue is placed behind the upper front teeth. This is how the posture is explained.

The most important point related to physical posture is our breath. Mind and breath are intimately connected; they go together. The breath follows wherever we focus the mind in meditation. If we try to settle the mind by suppressing it, it will obstruct the flow of the breath, which in turn will bring inner imbalance and even cause disease. It is therefore very important that we carefully investigate our breath at the beginning of the practice. We should observe the exhalation and inhalation as they occur, without manipulating the natural flow of our breath in any way. If we notice that our breath is audible, it indicates that it is too forceful. We should therefore relax it a bit more. Exhalation and inhalation should not be noticeable, as Kamalaśīla emphasizes.

In a sūtra it is stated that adopting the right posture in meditation will produce many wonderful results: states of meditative absorption will be quick to arise, one will be free of physical and mental hardships, and others will be inspired by faith. The faults of not adopting the seven-fold meditation posture and the benefits of doing so are explained in detail in the Lamdré teachings.

4. Nine methods to settle the mind

a. Placing the mind

In the Buddha's discourses, as well as in Maitreya's *Ornament of the Mahāyāna Sūtras*, nine methods to settle the mind are taught. The first method is called "placing the mind." It means to direct the mind towards the object of concentration and leave it there. In the Lamdré teachings this method is explained by means of four features: first, the object must be unmoving; second, one's body must be still; and third, the gaze must be unwavering, that is, the eyes are not blinking. Since the eyes contain the "channels of discursive thought," an unsteady gaze will stir up discursive thoughts. This might be difficult for beginners at first. Their eyes may tear up, but any initial discomfort will fade with practice. The fourth feature is that the object appears clearly in the mind. This is achieved by directing both the gaze and the mind on the blue flower or whatever focal support we are using. The object should then appear clearly in the mind.

It is usually said that the presence of three qualities determines a mind in meditative absorption: bliss, clarity, and non-conceptuality. However, bliss does not necessarily accompany every mind in absorption, because bliss is no longer experienced beyond the third level of concentration.[8] Nevertheless, the other two qualities of clarity and non-conceptuality must be there. From this we can understand why the object must be clear in the mind. In the same way, the mind must be free of discursive thinking to enter and abide in any level of absorption.

b. The five hindrances and their eight antidotes

It is taught in the sūtras that five faults, or hindrances, must be overcome for our meditation practice to be fruitful. This is accomplished by means of eight antidotes. These antidotes are called "conditioning factors," as they are in fact different mental factors that we must put to work in our practice.

The first hindrance is *laziness*, meaning not wanting to meditate or being reluctant to do so. Four antidotes are used to counteract laziness. The first is faith, or trust. In this context, *faith* is a clear appreciation of the practice of meditation based on the understanding of its immense benefits. Through the power of this clear appreciation of meditation arises the wish to practice it. This is the second antidote, called *eagerness*. When we have faith in the practice and the desire to engage in it, the third factor, *effort*, will arise and we will engage in the actual practice of meditation. The fourth factor counteracting laziness is called *pliancy*. When we sustain our effort in meditation with genuine interest, the mind will gradually become stable. If we persist in the practice based on this stability, the mind will eventually become well-trained and serviceable. This is pliancy. It is identified mainly as a mental factor. Until pliancy is achieved, one will encounter inner difficulties to sustaining the practice of meditation, as well as any other genuinely wholesome activity for that matter. But the moment it arises in the mind of a practitioner, all resistance subsides. This is the function of pliancy. Based on this mental state, there will be physical pliancy as well. This occurs when the energy winds move easily through the subtle channels in the body. The body will feel light and blissful and will lend itself well to the practice. The initial physical difficulties obstructing the practice of meditation, as well as the practice of wholesome deeds in general, is referred to as the negative tendency or coarseness of the body. When this is overcome through pliancy, meditation becomes pleasant and smooth. At this point, one can stay in meditation for a very long time, in fact, as long as one decides to, without any difficulties. This quality is physical pliancy. Generally, effort is said to be the cause for pliancy. However, since effort can be developed further based on pliancy, pliancy is also the cause for effort.

The second hindrance is *forgetting*. Its antidote is *remembering*,[9] that is, not forgetting the focal object of meditation. In this context, the terms *forgetting* and *remembering* take on a meaning that is slightly different from how they are commonly used. Let's say that we have chosen the blue flower as the focal support for our meditation. During the process of cultivating meditative concentration, we continually bring this flower to mind. Forgetting occurs the moment we lose focus and the flower is not held in mind, or remembered. In fact, meditation consists precisely of this faculty of remembering, or recollecting, the focal object. To meditate on the flower means that we do not allow the focus of our awareness to drift away from this object. This continuous recollection of the object is the actual essence of meditation.

The third fault or hindrance in concentration is called *sinking and agitation*. *Sinking* and *agitation* are two distinct mental factors which constitute the main obstacles during the actual practice of meditation. This is why they are mentioned together. *Sinking* means that the focal object is not clear in the mind. It is a form of drowsiness or mental lethargy, a lack of clear focus that makes the mind not serviceable. Sinking, drowsiness, and lack of clarity have the same meaning here. The second is agitation, which is different from distraction. Both are mental afflictions. *Distraction* refers to a mind that does not remain with the chosen wholesome object, whatever the wholesome object may be, but wanders off elsewhere. *Agitation* is defined more specifically as a mind not only distracted from the object of meditation, but that also follows an object of the five senses. Agitation occurs during our meditation or recitation practice when we think of a sense pleasure we have experienced in the past or fantasize about one we would like to experience in the future. It is therefore an aspect of the mental affliction of desirous attachment. The antidote for sinking and agitation is the mental factor of introspective awareness. It is an aspect of wisdom that, in the context of meditation, recognizes the hindrance present during meditation, knows which antidote is suitable to overcome it, and understands how to apply it. How does this unfold? After staying in meditation for a while and without interrupting the practice, we examine whether the mind is still focused on the chosen object or if it has wandered off to another object. This will allow us to understand how to settle the mind.

The fourth fault is called *non-application*. Non-application occurs when sinking or agitation are present during meditation, but instead of responding to them appropriately one leaves the mind as it is. In other words, it means not applying the antidotes, or not exerting the necessary effort. The antidote for this is *application*. The mental factor responsible here is *intention*, which is the factor that brings the main mind to the object. It is like a person who guides a king to a garden where he will enjoy various sights and smells. Similarly, when sinking or agitation occur, intention will lead the mind to their respective antidotes in order to apply them. When sinking is present to a small degree, it is sufficient to intensify one's focus. When the mind is only slightly agitated, distracted by an external perception for example, it must be brought back to the actual object of meditation. When neither of these occur, one should not bring their antidotes to mind, since this would be another mistake. When sinking or agitation are more powerful, we must rely on a variety of antidotes. In the case of overpowering drowsiness, we should interrupt the session and think about the amazing life stories of the buddhas and bodhisattvas. Once drowsiness is dispelled in this way, we resume the cultivation of concentration with renewed inspiration for the practice. When the mind is distracted by strong agitation, we should think about our own death and impermanence. This will produce a sense of dissatisfaction and weariness that will dispel agitation. Once it is dispelled in this way, we can resume the practice with renewed diligence.

The fifth fault is the *excessive application* of antidotes. Once we have recognized the hindrance, whether sinking or agitation, overcome it through the application of appropriate antidotes, and brought the mind back to the object of meditation, it is no longer necessary to employ any antidotes. If we continue to bring the antidotes to mind instead of just remaining with the object at this point, it will stir up unnecessary thinking. The antidote for excessive application is *balanced application* or equanimity." The term *equanimity* can have a variety of meanings. Here, it refers to the mental factor that allows the mind to relax and settle down. It allows us to remain with the focal object, free of sinking and agitation.

c. The remaining eight methods to settle the mind

Some teachers explain these methods as the sequential stages of practice occurring one after the other. The second method is "continuous placement." This method consists not merely of placing the mind on the object, but of staying with it for an extended period of time. The third method is called "repairing and placing": when we notice that the mind has left the focal object, we stop it and bring it back. The fourth is "close placement": when the mind repeatedly strays away, we bring it back to the object over and over again.

The fifth is called "subduing." This method helps us overcome resistance to the practice that may occur when the body or the mind become tired during meditation. When we feel that we do not want to practice any longer, we should recall the extraordinary benefits of the practice and persist. To overcome resistance to meditation in this way is called "subduing." The sixth is "pacifying": when the mind in meditation is troubled by a surge of thoughts and afflictions for example, we stop and think about the faults and undesired consequences of distraction, and then resume the practice once these troublemakers are pacified. The seventh method is called "pacifying thoroughly": when the obstacle of sinking and agitation, or any disruptive thought for that matter, occurs for just a moment, we immediately recognize it as a fault and then resume the practice.

The first four of the nine methods to settle the mind allow us to bring the mind to the object of meditation. The next three are the methods used to overcome obstacles that occur while the mind focuses one-pointedly on the object. Methods eight and nine are the results of training in meditation or samādhi.

The eighth is called "making the mind one-pointed": through deliberate focus, the mind remains with one-pointed attention on the object for as long as one wants. The ninth is called "perfectly balanced attention": by training in this way, the mind will eventually remain fully attentive to the chosen object without any deliberate effort. At this point the mind can effortlessly remain in equipoise, in meditation and also during daily activities, such as eating, walking, sitting, and so forth.

Three kinds of mind can generally be distinguished: the mind of the desire realm, the mind of the form realm, and the mind of the formless realm. The mental stability of the ninth method to settle the mind is called "one-pointedness of the desire realm." In other words, it is not a genuine samādhi of the actual four levels of meditative concentration or of the four formless absorptions. Having said that, it is extremely beneficial to cultivate it because this one-pointedness will eventually generate mental pliancy, based on which the genuine state of calm abiding will arise. This state of calm abiding then becomes the genuine form realm mind. Künkhyen Gorampa explained that the one-pointed mind of the desire realm must possess a certain level of mental pliancy. We must add, however, that the mind of the desire realm does not have strong calm abiding. When pliancy is strong, however, this is what is called "calm abiding." It was taught thus in the sūtras.

5. Worldly calm abiding and beyond

Beyond calm abiding, we must also cultivate profound insight. The practice of calm abiding is known in Hindu traditions as well and is not exclusive to the Buddhist tradition. This practice involves a certain type of worldly wisdom explained as the path that takes calm abiding as its support. It is referred to as "wisdom endowed with the aspect of unrefined calmness."[10] This path has four levels in the form realm, four in the formless realm, and one in the desire realm, making a total of nine levels. On the basis of the mind of calm abiding, this wisdom endowed with the aspect of unrefined calmness recognizes each of the respectively higher levels as sublime and every level below its current level as inferior. By cultivating this wisdom, the mind progresses through the nine levels and is thus able to eliminate the coarse afflictions of the three realms, except for those of the peak of existence.[11] To achieve this, one uses what are called the "seven reflections" related to one's practice of calm abiding. On each level, these reflections enable us to eliminate the afflictions of the immediately preceding lower level and to attain the next higher level.

If, in addition to calm abiding, we also cultivate the profound insight that knows the reality of no-self, we will be able to attain the fruition of the three vehicles, that is, the level of an arhat, of a pratyekabuddha, or of a fully awakened buddha. This means that the genuine practice of liberating insight also takes the various levels of calm abiding as its support.

6. Some practical instructions

The most crucial practical instructions for meditation we should always keep in mind are the following: "At first, intensify; in the middle, relax; finally, intensify and relax as appropriate. Eventually, leave it as it is." If we do not intensify our focus at the beginning, we will not be able to interrupt the continuous arising of thoughts. Thus, by intensifying the focus, our attention will remain with the object and will not drift away. The mind will not be occupied with thoughts other than the object of meditation. Once the mind stays with the object, the focus should be somewhat relaxed. This is the meaning of *In the middle, relax*. If we relax it too much, however, it will begin to sink and become drowsy. When this happens, we again intensify the focus; and then we relax it again, and so on. In this way, we adapt the quality of our attention, intensifying and relaxing the focus as appropriate. This is the meaning of *Finally, intensify and relax as appropriate*. Eventually, the mind will remain with the focal object, free of sinking and agitation, in a state of clear, nonconceptual attention. At this point, we just let it be without interfering. This is the meaning of *Eventually, leave it as it is*.

When we first begin with the practice of calm abiding, it is important that we keep the sessions short. If the sessions are too long and we are not able to meditate well, we will generate aversion towards the practice and will lose the desire to meditate. Therefore, it is enough to have sessions of no more than five minutes at a time in the beginning and then repeat such short sessions a few times. Gradually we can lengthen the duration of each session.

The Lamdré teachings on the three perceptions speak of five experiences we go through in the process of cultivating calm abiding.[12] First is the experience of recognizing thoughts: we directly experience the incessant surge of discourse thoughts welling up in the mind during meditation. This is a genuine meditative experience. This great stream of thoughts was there even before we started meditating, but it was not recognized as such. Now, we see it for what it is. If we continue to meditate, we will be able to remain with the object of meditation for a short while before the stream of thoughts resumes. This is the second experience called the experience of the resting of thoughts: short intermittent periods of focused attention in meditation. If we then persist in the practice, these moments of undistracted attention will become increasingly longer, though they are still interrupted by the sudden arising of thoughts. This is the third type of experience called tired thoughts. Fourth is the experience of waves of thought. By diligently persisting in this way, we are now able to pacify thoughts as soon as they arise and then remain focused on the object of meditation for an extended period. The fifth experience is called pacified thoughts. By sustaining the continuity of attention in this way, all thoughts will eventually be pacified and the mind will remain focused on the object with great clarity and without the need to exert any effort. This experience is equivalent to the eighth and ninth methods to settle the mind discussed above.

II. The Perfection of Wisdom

A. What is Wisdom?

We will now discuss the last of the six perfections, the perfection of wisdom. Wisdom is defined as a mind that knows the true nature of things. If this wisdom is imbued with bodhicitta and so forth,[13] it becomes a cause for attaining the state of complete buddhahood, the fruition of the Mahāyāna path. This wisdom is then called the perfection of wisdom.

The factor opposing wisdom is ignorance or delusion, which is the aspect of our mind that does not know the true nature of things. What are the faults or undesirable consequences of lacking wisdom? Even from a worldly perspective, people understand the disadvantages of ignorance and the benefits of knowledge, and so many spend their whole lives studying to accumulate knowledge. Those who do not develop their knowledge will find it difficult to live happily and to avoid problems in their lives. If we don't know how to accomplish our work, whatever it may be, we will not be able to accomplish it successfully. In terms of the path of Dharma, since we have not familiarized ourselves with the practice up until now, it is impossible to succeed on the path without learning the Dharma first.

The most important aspect of wisdom is the wisdom that knows the reality of no-self, or selflessness. This wisdom is the only antidote to ignorance that will allow us to uproot self-grasping and to relinquish the mental afflictions. Thus, as long we lack the wisdom of selflessness it is impossible to attain true freedom from saṃsāra, not to mention the attainment of buddhahood. It is taught that to follow the path to liberation we must have the foundation of ethical discipline and gradually train ourselves through hearing, reflection, and meditation. Studies are therefore indispensable. This does not mean, however, that we must spend an excessive amount of time studying. Master Buddhaguhya stated that both excessive learning and insufficient knowledge are obstacles for the path.

Buddhahood is the perfect accomplishment of the qualities of relinquishment and realization. The relinquishment of obscurations is achieved through wisdom and the realization of excellent qualities is accomplished through the method aspect of the path, such as generosity and so forth. Furthermore, the achievement of wisdom requires the help of the method aspect and method is assisted by wisdom. In this way, method and wisdom support each other.

Moreover, each of the six perfections is greater than the previous one. The difference between one perfection and the next is said to be as vast as the difference between the amount of water collected in a cow's hoof print and the water gathered in an ocean. Since wisdom is the last of the six perfections, it is the most sublime of them all. However, buddhahood cannot be attained through wisdom alone. This supreme accomplishment absolutely requires both method and wisdom. Śāntideva explains that the first five perfections are the necessary conditions for wisdom to arise. Among those five, the most important condition is concentration. The specific cause for profound insight is to have heard the teachings extensively.

B. How is Wisdom Cultivated?

In his commentary on the instructions on *Parting from the Four Attachments*, Gorampa states that generally the cultivation of insight is taught by means of two methods: meditation on the selflessness of the individual and meditation on the selflessness of phenomena. In the tradition of these teachings, however, insight is cultivated in meditation by means of three key points: establishing that appearances are mind, that mind is illusory, and that the illusory is devoid of inherent nature. In post-meditation, the view is cultivated by seeing things as illusory. He then goes on to say that even conceptually "selflessness," or "emptiness," is very difficult to understand. Furthermore, the path of meditation on emptiness is riddled with pitfalls and can go wrong in many places, and it is impossible to gain a clear understanding of it based on the written word alone. Gorampa therefore does not discuss the subject in detail in this commentary, but he gives some advice that will be of immediate benefit to us. He says that when we accomplish wholesome deeds, we should not cling to notions like "I am a good person" or "This is an excellent deed I accomplished." Our practice should not be corrupted by such thoughts, clinging to the agent and the action as truly existent. Instead, we should think "All of this is not real; it is illusory!" This will be very beneficial.

C. The Dangers of Teaching "Emptiness"

Teaching emptiness can be very dangerous. If we explain this profound subject to someone new to Buddhism and say things like "all phenomena are emptiness," they will not comprehend. They might misunderstand what we are saying to mean that nothing exists and therefore think that this teaching is complete nonsense. Instead of generating faith in the profound teaching on emptiness, they might develop aversion, which is a great obstacle to their path. Thus, the danger in teaching emptiness is that we might inadvertently create conditions that will prevent others from generating faith in the Dharma, which, in turn, will prevent them from practicing the liberating path. Another serious danger is that people might misunderstand "emptiness," thinking that it means that there is no law of cause and effect, and therefore that our actions have no consequences. This misunderstanding will generate a nihilistic worldview and other mistaken ideas.

It is therefore crucial that the teacher clearly explains the principles of karma, the law of actions and their results, before talking about this profound matter. In fact, it is taught that introducing emptiness to someone who is not ready for these teachings is a root transgression of the bodhisattva vow, a violation that will result in rebirth in the hell realm.

D. Approaches to Selflessness and the Two Realities

There are two principal approaches to the meditative cultivation of insight into selflessness, or emptiness: for those who have a vast knowledge of the scriptures and for those who have not studied them extensively. Here, I will combine both approaches.

In terms of the method of practice, we can distinguish two main systems. According to the first, insight into the two types of selflessness[14] is cultivated simultaneously, whereas the other system develops this insight gradually. Within the sequential approach, there are again many different methods: some begin by establishing appearances as mind, others do not. Here, we will begin by discussing the method that does not establish appearances as mind.

To be able to successfully cultivate insight into emptiness, it is first necessary to develop an understanding of the two realities: relative and ultimate. Even though we speak of two "realities," only one of them—the ultimate—is real, the other is false. The term *relative reality* comprises everything the mind can take as its object. The ultimate lies beyond the scope of our mind. The function of conceptual analysis is therefore limited: it can bring us closer to a genuine understanding, but it cannot reach the ultimate itself. Those who have achieved direct perception of the ultimate are called āryas, or noble beings. The term *ultimate reality* is therefore the name given to that which is directly perceived by the wisdom of an ārya in meditative equipoise. From this, we can understand that the statement "all phenomena are emptiness," found in the Perfection of Wisdom Sūtras, is not true from all perspectives. From the perspective of ultimate truth, everything is indeed emptiness, and it is from this standpoint that phenomena are said to be nonexistent. From the conventional perspective of ordinary beings, however, things are real. In this sense we can say that things exist from the perspective of relative truth and that they do not exist from the perspective of ultimate truth.

E. The Two Types of Selflessness

The term *individual* in the expression "selflessness of the individual" means sentient being, like me, you, he, she, and so forth. *Phenomena* in "selflessness of phenomena" denotes the phenomena of the outer environment except for beings, such as mountains, lakes, houses, food, clothes, and so on, as well the inner phenomena constituting a sentient being, such as the eyes, the ears, and so forth.

The term *self of the individual* refers to the truly existent identity of the individual, and *self of phenomena* to the truly existent identity of phenomena. "Selflessness of the individual" therefore refers to the emptiness or lack of true existence in the individual and "selflessness of phenomena" to the emptiness or lack of true existence in phenomena. This is also the meaning of the phrase "phenomena are emptiness."

1. The self of the individual

a. Searching for the self

The individual, or "person," is the notion "I" conceptually imputed on the basis of the six elements. The six elements are the element of earth, comprising the body's hard parts, such the flesh and bones, and so on; the element of water, such the blood, urine, and pus; the element of fire, which is the body's warmth; the element of wind, the breath; the element of space, which are the cavities of the body, such the cavities in the nostrils; and the element of consciousness, which is the mind.

Once we have identified these constituent parts of the individual, we begin to search for the "I" or "self" we conceptually cling to by investigating whether it exists among any of the six elements. We do this step by step, beginning with an analysis of the earth element: "Is the self identical to the teeth or not?" Searching in this way, we will see that the teeth and the self are not the same. If they were identical, the characteristics of the self must also apply to the teeth. First, we think of ourselves as being a single and whole being. Second, we believe this "I" or self to be permanent, fundamentally unchanging over time. And third, we think that we are in control of the body, including the teeth. The self is therefore believed to be autonomous. These three characteristics of the self—i.e., being a single unit, permanent, and autonomous—do not apply to the teeth. Since there are many teeth, the characteristic of being unitary does not apply. If each tooth had its own self, one person would have multiple selves. The same applies to the hair, of which we have much more than teeth.

This type of analysis is then repeated to investigate the existence of the self in each of the other elements comprising the individual, up to consciousness. In this way, we come to see that all of these elements share the characteristic of being multiple, as opposed to unitary, impermanent, as opposed to permanent, and under the control of other elements, as opposed to autonomous. The self is therefore fundamentally different from all the elements based on which it is imputed. Following this analysis, we will understand that there is no self.

b. Applying the view in meditation

Once we have a good theoretical understanding of the nonexistence of the self, we must apply this view in meditation. For this, we use the same methods discussed earlier in the context of calm abiding. Instead of a flower or a buddha image, we now make the view of profound insight the focal object of our meditation. This means that we first go through the analysis outlined above until we come to the conclusion that the self does not exist, and then familiarize ourselves with the view by remaining focused on this thought.

When the view of no-self is cultivated in this way on the basis of the mind of calm abiding, we speak of the union of calm abiding and profound insight. The view that understands the true nature of things is likened to the flame of a candle and the stability of calm abiding to a protective shield. The union of calm abiding and profound insight is then the steady flame of insight undisturbed by the winds of discursive thought.

Some teachers have stated that calm abiding is the aspect of unwavering focus on one focal object, and that profound insight is the aspect of the conceptual analysis that investigates the many reasons why the self of the individual does not exist. According to their understanding, the mind that remains focused on the view after the analysis is by definition the mind of calm abiding and not profound insight. Others have refuted this understanding, explaining that the sūtras speak of two types of profound insight: the insight of discerning awareness engaged in analysis and unwavering insight, which does not actively investigate. The insight that uses analytical reasoning is the preparatory stage for the formal practice used before settling the mind in one-pointed concentration on the view, and it can also be cultivated during post-meditation. Unwavering insight is the non-conceptual awareness placed in the view of emptiness without wavering from it during the main practice in meditative equipoise.

c. The self and the five skandhas

Another approach to the selflessness of the individual is based on an analysis of the five skandhas. For this, we must first know the five skandhas. They are the five groups of phenomena—form and so forth—constituting an individual being, like ourselves. The skandha of form includes our eyes, ears, nose, tongue, and body—that is, our five sense faculties, as well as their respective objects, that is, visual forms, sounds, smells, tastes, and objects of touch. Besides these ten, an eleventh form is sometimes mentioned.[15] When we speak of the five sense faculties of the eyes, ears, and so on, we are not referring to the eyeballs or the outer ears which we can see with our eyes. These are classified as the sense objects. The sense faculties are the subtle matter inside these physical organs that has the potential to give rise to the corresponding sense consciousness.

The skandha of sensation refers to the pleasant, unpleasant, and neutral sensations we experience. The skandha of perception is a particular mental factor. Every phenomenon has its own characteristic features that distinguish it from other phenomena. That which apprehends these particular features is the mental factor of perception. The skandha of formative factors, or formations, comprises two types: concomitant formations and non-concomitant formations. Concomitant formations are the forty-nine or fifty-one mental factors that arise in our mind,[16] including unwholesome states like desire, wholesome states like faith, and others. Non-concomitant formations are phenomena like words, phrases, past, future, and so on.[17] Lastly, the skandha of consciousness is the mind.

The self is conceived of on the basis of these five skandhas. In other words, we apprehend the skandhas as the self. It is precisely this relationship between the skandhas we cling to and the self we identify with that we must investigate. The skandhas and the self must either be one and the same or different entities. When we look at the matter from this perspective, we first come to realize that they are not the same, because their defining characteristics are incompatible. The skandhas are multiple and impermanent by nature, whereas the self is conceived as being an unchanging, single identity. But at the same time, they also cannot be separate entities. We only ever think of "I" in relation to these skandhas. We never identify with outer phenomena, like a house or a tree. When we analyze it in this way, we can never find this self. Therefore, we say that ultimately there is no self. Conventionally, there is something called "self" or "I" that is conceptually posited on the basis of our individual skandhas, just as we give the label "house" to an assemblage of walls, a roof, a door, and windows. Both these labels are created by the mind and superimposed on a collection of phenomena.

2. The self of phenomena

a. Examining phenomena by means of reasoning

The lack of inherent identity in phenomena can be established in the same way, as well as through many other types of reasoning. One line of reasoning called "vajra slivers" investigates the arising of phenomena from the perspective of the cause. Every functioning entity arises from causes and conditions. In other words, there are no entities that are not born from causes and conditions. Though this may seem obvious, we must investigate whether the way we relate to the arising of a given phenomenon corresponds to reality. There are four possible ways of arising to examine, based on the four possible relationships between the result and its cause: (1) Does the result arise from a cause that is identical to the result? (2) Does it arise from a cause that is a different, separate entity? (3) Does it arise from a cause that is both identical and different? Or (4) does it arise without a cause?

1. In the first case, if a resultant phenomenon were to arise from a cause identical to itself, then the result would arise from itself. However, if a phenomenon that arises from itself is not already present, it cannot be brought into existence through other conditions, and if it already exists, it is meaningless to speak of its arising.

2. In the second case, if a result could arise from a cause that is different from itself, then a lion cub could be born from an elephant, which is of course impossible.[18]

3. The third case implies a contradiction, since two things cannot be inherently the same and different at the same time.

4. Lastly, the fourth possibility of arising—namely the arising of a result without a cause—is an absurd position to hold.

Even common people understand that results arise from causes and conditions, and they work hard on the causes that will produce desired results. This is obvious. Through this reasoning in four steps, we come to understand that there is no arising of a result from a cause.

Another line of reasoning investigates the process of arising from the perspective of the result. This analysis is called "refuting the arising of an existent and a nonexistent thing." When a result is born from a cause, is this result existent at the time of the cause or is it nonexistent at that time? If it already exists at the time of the cause, its arising would be redundant; and if it does not exist, then nothing could ever bring it into existence.

Yet another line of reasoning—called "neither one nor many"—investigates the essence of things, both causes and results alike. The ordinary mind perceives things as singular entities. By questioning whether this perception corresponds to reality, we come to understand that phenomena do not exist in the way we conceive them. According to the two lower Buddhist tenet systems—Vaibhāṣika and Sautrāntika—the subtle particles that constitute the smallest constituents of physical matter are partless units that cannot be further divided into smaller elements. However, according to the two higher Buddhist tenet systems—Cittamātra and Madhyamaka—these particles are not indivisible; they are composed of many smaller parts. If one particle of matter is surrounded by ten other particles in each of its ten directions, we can conceptually distinguish a central part of the particle and ten directional parts, each connected to one of these other ten particles. Thus, a so-called "partless particle" becomes a particle with many parts, and we can therefore no longer speak of a "unit." Without "units" the notion of "many" makes no sense, since "many" denotes the gathering of multiple "units." If there are no real units and multiplicities, all phenomena become nonexistent.

Beyond the three lines of reasoning explained so far, there is a fourth type called "the reasoning of dependent arising." It investigates all entities and non-entities. All compounded phenomena arise in dependence of causes and conditions. That being so, there is no arising of phenomena in the ultimate sense. When we see our reflection in the mirror, for instance, the reflection can only appear when all the causes and conditions, such as the presence of the face, the mirror, and so forth, are aligned. To say "there is no arising" means, in this case, that there is no reflection unless all the causes and conditions for it are present. In this sense, we say that phenomena are not truly existent.

Based on these lines of reasoning, we establish the view that understands the reality of non-arising, that is, emptiness. Once this understanding reaches a high degree of certainty, we place our awareness directly in this view that all phenomena are emptiness. The moment emptiness is realized directly, self-grasping along with the other afflictions present in our mind are eliminated. In this way, we are able to accomplish the resultant state of a śrāvaka arhat. Loving kindness, compassion, and all the other practices pertaining to the method aspect of the path can reduce the strength of anger and so forth, but they cannot eliminate the seeds of these afflictions from our mindstream. To relinquish these seeds we need the wisdom that realizes selflessness.

b. Emptiness beyond nonexistence

We could now ask whether the selflessness and the reality of non-arising explained above are the fundamental nature of phenomena. The answer to this question would be: No, they are not. The fundamental nature must be the ultimate reality of things, whereas the selflessness and the non-arising discussed so far are conventional realities fabricated by conceptual thought. It is like the notions of "long" and "short," which are created by thought in dependence on each other: without "long" there is no "short" and vice versa. Similarly, there is no "over here" without "over there," and no "good" without "bad." All these categories are established by thought. In the same way, the notions of "emptiness," "selflessness," "non-arising," and so forth are also established in dependence on the concepts of "non-emptiness," "self," and "arising." Without objects to be negated—i.e., "self," "arising," and so forth—the notions that negate them, such as "selflessness" and "non-arising," cannot be established. Based on this reasoning we can understand that not only the notions of "self," "arising," and so forth must be negated, but "selflessness" and "non-arising" as well. This is the second stage in the search for the fundamental nature of things.

After negating the arising and the non-arising of phenomena in this way, we may wonder whether the fundamental nature of things could consist of their combination. However, since there is neither "arising" nor "non-arising," the combination "arising and non-arising" is impossible. This is the third stage of negation.

Finally, we may ask whether the fundamental nature is the nonexistence of both arising and non-arising. This is also not the case, since this too is a conceptual elaboration based on the notion "arising and non-arising." The fundamental nature of things is beyond the four extremes. It is free of all elaborations. It is not the object of conceptual thought. It cannot be expressed with words. It is nothing that could be pinpointed in any way, and this is precisely what is conventionally labeled "the fundamental nature of things."

Following these lines of reasoning, we first develop certainty based on logical analysis. Then, we must familiarize ourselves with the result of the analysis in meditation. How is this done? Once we have understood that the fundamental nature of things is free from all four extremes, we settle in this view without distraction and without fabricating anything mentally. In other words, we remain in a state without refuting or establishing anything.

F. Pith Instructions for Insight

The meditation instructions for profound insight explained up to this point can be rather difficult to apply for those who have not studied the great Buddhist philosophical treatises. In the tradition of the teachings on *Parting from the Four Attachments*, pith instructions are used to establish the view. Here, the meditation on the selflessness of the individual is not taught separately from the meditation on the selflessness of phenomena. The method to develop insight into both types of selflessness uses analogies, such as the dream, the TV screen, or the magical illusion. In our dreams, we can see ourselves and other people. Similarly, different beings can appear on a TV screen, and magicians can generate illusions in the form of human beings and so forth. In all of these instances, beings appear, but even though they are seen, they do not really exist. Similarly, even though we have the appearances of ourselves and others in our waking lives, they all lack true existence. This is the first reflection we should familiarize ourselves with to establish that appearances are mind.

1. Establishing appearances as mind

To establish that everything that appears to our present awareness—all forms, sounds, smells, etc.—is mind, eight analogies are given. One of these is the analogy of the dream. Under the influence of sleep, we dream of ourselves, of those close to us, and so forth. All these people appear in our dreams, but they are not real: as soon as we wake up, they are all gone. In just the same way, beings appear to us in our waking lives under the influence of ignorance. Yet as soon as we wake up from the slumber of ignorance, we realize that they never really existed. By familiarizing ourselves with this reflection, we develop an understanding of the selflessness of the individual according to the pith instructions.

The exact same method applies to the appearances of objects such as forms and smells: just as these objects appear in our dreams but do not really exist, they also appear in our waking lives but are devoid of true existence. All these things are merely mental appearances. In other words, they are mind. Once this understanding is ascertained, we must familiarize ourselves with it with focused attention. This is how we meditate on the lack of true existence of the objects of perception through pith instructions.

2. Establishing mind as illusory

We may then ask "If, in the end, all appearances are mind, is the mind real?" This too is not the case. To establish that the mind too does not truly exist but is illusory, the pith instructions again use eight analogies, one of which is the analogy of illusion. With the help of certain techniques and props, a master illusionist can make beings and objects such as a house appear, but even though they appear, these things are not real. By reflecting on this analogy and familiarizing ourselves with its meaning, we can establish that the mind—that which apprehends objects—is devoid of true existence.

3. Establishing the illusory as devoid of inherent nature

What is left at this point, after the objects of perception and the perceiving mind have been established as lacking true existence? Only the mere luminosity of the mind. The various schools of thought explain it in different ways. In the Mahāyāna tradition it is termed "universal ground consciousness," and in non-Buddhist traditions it is sometimes referred to as the "self." By understanding that this luminosity is devoid of inherent nature through the third stage of these pith instructions, it too is established as lacking true existence. Two reflections are used here: dependent arising and inexpressibility. From the perspective of relative reality, the mind is explained to arise in dependence. From the perspective of ultimate reality, it is said to be inexpressible.

One of the eight analogies used to teach the dependent arising of the mere luminosity of the mind is the analogy of recitation. When a teacher teaches their students the recitation of the homage formula, they will first say the words "Namo buddhāya," and the students will repeat "Namo buddhāya." When this happens, it is not the case that the words pronounced by the teacher are transferred to the students. The students' recitation occurs in dependence on the teacher's words. Since they have dependently arisen, they lack true arising. The inexpressible nature of the mind's mere luminosity is identical to the freedom from elaborations discussed above in the context of the objects of perception. Here, it is explained from the perspective of the subject.

Even though an ārya's actual direct experience of reality free from all elaborations cannot be clearly communicated by means of words, saying "This is it!", it is explained by means of analogies, such as the analogy of a child's laughter. When a baby that cannot yet speak laughs, it has its reason, but it cannot say what it is. The ārya's direct experience is said to be like that.

Some teachers claim that emptiness cannot be correctly understood through analogies and that we must resort to logical reasoning. They strongly emphasize this point, stating that there is indeed no other way except for conceptual analysis. This is not correct, however. Not only is it possible to understand emptiness through analogies, but this knowledge can also arise on the basis of the words of the Buddha. This was explained in detail by the great omniscient master Rongtön.

To conclude your meditation session on the view, dedicate the merit generated in this way and recite prayers of aspirations. As you leave your meditation seat and go outside, think that everyone you meet appears yet does not really exist, like an illusion.

This completes the main part of these teachings.

Concluding Words of Advice

Since this ten-day Dharma course was widely announced, many people have come here from abroad. I am truly glad about this and would like to thank everyone for their sincere efforts in their studies here. I also thank the translators and all the staff of IBA for their hard work in organizing this program. We also had many students from shedras in India as well as from Tibet, and I would like to thank them too for attending these teachings.

I would now like to address a few words to those who teach and study at the shedras.[19] For a long time now, khenpos, teachers, and students of our shedras have been engaged in expounding and listening to the Dharma. These are the activities directly related to the teachings of the Buddha and it is the conduct of sublime beings. I deeply rejoice in this and compliment you for your commitment. This kind of work is actually very difficult. Both teachers and students have to put forth a lot of effort, spending many hours every day preparing for lectures and reviewing what has been taught. This is not easy. It is very different from physical work. Year after year, the Dharma is being transmitted despite these difficulties. Again, thank you so much for your efforts in this regard.

Following the example of our teacher, the Buddha Śākyamuni, the monastic students have laid down activities for this life, have taken ordination, observe ethical discipline, and study the great treatises. We should know that this is precisely the path followed by the buddhas of the three times. How absolutely wonderful! I deeply rejoice in this.

In terms of the procedure followed in the studies, the khenpos first give instructions on the scriptures, the students study them on their own, and then they engage in formal debates based on these texts. In this way, they gain a solid understanding of the scriptures. But the studies do not stop there. There are many other means to develop our knowledge, for instance, by praising our root gurus, that is, the lamas from whom we have received empowerments. In fact, once we have received an empowerment from a lama, we should not critically observe their behavior, but train in perceiving them as actual buddhas. This will be of great benefit for our understanding of the Dharma. After the Lord of Dharma Sakya Paṇḍita received the guru yoga transmission from Drakpa Gyaltsen, he viewed his lama as Mañjughoṣa in person and a genuine inner realization was born in him. In this way, he was able to become learned in all fields of knowledge and was highly respected by everyone. He himself stated that this will happen to anyone who practices in this way. Devotion for one's teacher is therefore very helpful for one's understanding of the Dharma. If possible, we should respect those who teach and explain the Dharma to us as equals to the Buddha. At the very least, we should not upset them in any way.

In the same way, we should treat our Dharma friends and the Dharma itself with respect. This too will benefit our studies greatly. It is sometimes said that some people fail to gain a solid understanding of the texts during their formal studies. However, if they learn these texts after having spent a few years in retreat, they can develop excellent understanding. This is true, because the practices of confession and purification will enable our intelligence to grasp the teachings more readily. If we cannot devote time to practice in retreat during our studies, we can still develop our aptitude by learning the seven-limb practice well and performing it at least three times every day. It is an excellent method that combines the three aspects of confession, purification, and increase, which will benefit our understanding of the scriptures. I therefore strongly encourage you to take up this practice.

The next point I would like to mention is the crucial importance of actively developing our motivation. To speak from my own experience, when I was a student, I didn't think that this was the time to work on my motivation and to practice, and I disregarded these aspects. The lamas, however, always instructed us to generate the motivation of bodhicitta. They advised us, saying that to lead all beings to happiness and the causes of happiness, we must first listen to the Dharma and then put the teachings into practice. It is said that when both the teacher and the student generate such good motivation, every Dharma lesson will produce immeasurable merit. In this way, our study sessions become a form of practice and a very powerful wholesome activity. The importance of generating the right motivation when we study can therefore hardly be overstated.

The same is true for the practice of debate. The Great Butön said that if we debate with the intention for ourselves to win and for our debate partner to lose, then it becomes an unwholesome action. It is said that in one of their previous lives, when our teacher the Buddha and Mañjuśrī were still on the path, they once held a long debate. One defended the position that all phenomena exist and the other that they do not exist. In the end, nothing good came from this debate. It is therefore important to appreciate that debate is a form of study and to turn it into a Dharma practice. If we study with the motivation to become learned so that we can teach all subjects, the true blessings of the Dharma will not penetrate our being. But if we learn the Dharma in order to practice it, not only will we receive its full blessings, but we will also understand it in a more complete way. I therefore encourage you all to act accordingly.

Another important point to keep in mind is the potential danger we may run into as students of the philosophical treatises and textbooks. When we divide the various Indian and Tibetan Buddhist schools of thought into "those that belong to us" and "the others," we may be led to think that we do not need to know the tenets of the "other traditions." To generate dislike for these traditions in this way is a grave mistake. When I first studied Madhyamaka, I learned that a certain teacher stated that it was wrong to assert that the teachings of the Mahāyāna would become meaningless if the subject of selflessness was also taught in the scriptures of the Hīnayāna. That teacher turned out to be the master Bhāvaviveka. As a result, I thought that Bhāvaviveka was a very bad teacher indeed. This generated a serious negative karma. The masters of these "other" traditions are all great bodhisattvas. In terms of objects in relation to which we generate karma, bodhisattvas are of exceptional significance. We must therefore be very mindful about the way we relate to them.

Being biased is not a problem exclusive to the students of philosophy, however. Taktsang Lotsāwa explained that a biased attitude in relation to the Dharma is a source of many faults for anyone who holds such views. It will turn the Dharma, for us, into a support for jealousy, competitiveness, and so on. We are not only missing the point; we are accumulating serious negative karma. It amounts to the fault of abandoning the Dharma. In this way, being biased in relation to the Dharma will impair our roots of goodness. It will cause our faith and devotion to be partial and limited. In other words, we will be unable to develop pervasive devotion. In brief, approaching the one Dharma of the Buddha in this way, we divide it into two fractions: our side versus the side of others. This will generate jealousy and competitiveness, which in turn will engender negative karma. What a senseless, regrettable thing to do! We should therefore make a strong resolve to completely abandon such behavior.

How are we to achieve this? In this regard, Dezhung Choktrul Rinpoche advised that one should practice in accordance with one's own tradition, while at the same time cultivating faith in and pure perception of all other traditions. We should be very clear about this and completely determined to maintain such an open-minded view.

Teachers can have a great impact on the minds and attitudes of their students. Their sole concern should be that these students have benefited by the time they leave the shedra and that their time there was not wasted. When teachers devise a curriculum and a lesson plan based on such an intention, the outcome will be excellent, and it will determine the students' progress in their studies. This should be the teachers' main concern.

A task that both teachers and senior students should share is concern for younger students. It is always good to check in with them, inquire about their well-being, and make sure they are being looked after well. If they need help, offer it to them, and correct them in their conduct. This support is very important, especially the point of helping them with their outer discipline. Even for ordinary tasks, if we are asked to help someone, we must first check whether we should or should not offer our support. If there are valid reasons to do so, it is of course good to help. It would be absurd to remain idle in such a situation. We should help others as much as we are able to and do so voluntarily, without having to be assigned that task by others. I humble request all of you to behave in this way.

There is one final point I would like to make. After having completed your studies, I urge you all to sincerely put your knowledge into practice. The Lord of Dharma Sakya Paṇḍita said that there are two main activities for scholars. Once one has become learned, he says, one should either engage in explaining the Dharma to others or pursue the path of practice. We should know, however, that for whomever chooses the former, the first step is to study to become learned in the teachings, and then to follow the correct sequence of practicing them oneself before starting to teach others. In other words, it is not appropriate to instruct others without having gone through the practice oneself. It is not actually wrong to teach without having practiced first, but it would be the opposite of the prescribed sequence. At any rate, the point I want to emphasize here is that it is very important for everyone to engage in the practice.

These days, it is difficult to find the circumstances to practice in retreat, and in particular the tradition of meditation seems to be in decline. I was therefore delighted to hear that there are currently more than two hundred practitioners in Lamdré retreat in the Kau Ritrö hermitage of Dzongsar. We really need this kind of activity. If, beginning today, we sincerely strive to tame our mind, we will be able to subdue it. Then our studies will not be wasted. In other words, putting the Dharma we have learned into practice is the very meaning of not wasting our time. We should therefore pledge to engage in sincere practice. It is important that our practice of meditation is based on this kind of reason. I request you all to make the strong resolve to study well, reflect well, and meditate well. Please keep this mind.

Many people have come here to listen to the Dharma and we have been your hosts here. For some of the monastics here, the conditions where not ideal, and I would like to apologize for this.

Over the past few days, we have generated great wholesome potential by explaining and listening to the Dharma, and it is important to dedicate this properly, so that these actions become the cause for the attainment of buddhahood.

By this merit may we attain omniscience.
Defeating the foe, wrongdoing,
May we liberate beings from the ocean of existence,
Disturbed by the waves of birth, old age, sickness, and death.

Endnotes

Introduction

1. This period saw the establishment of important monasteries, like Samyé in Central Tibet, the founding of scholastic and monastic lineages, and the translation of important Buddhist texts, all initially under royal patronage.
2. The empire gradually collapsed after the assassination of King Ralpachen by his younger brother Langdarma, who famously persecuted monastics and destroyed Buddhist institutions. Just a few years after his ascension to the throne, Langdarma was himself assassinated, and what once was a unified empire disintegrated into a cluster of kingdoms ruled by local aristocratic families. Paradoxically, this political instability and decentralization created fertile ground for religious innovation, with the rulers of different regions supporting different Buddhist traditions.
3. These are the Hevajra Tantra and the two commentarial tantras, i.e., *Samputatantra* and *Vajrapañjaratantra*.
4. The most comprehensive collection of these teachings was compiled by Müchen Sempa Chenpo Könchok Gyaltsen, translated and published by Thubten Jinpa as *Mind Training: The Great Collection*. See the bibliography for further details.
5. For a commentary on this text see Khenchen Appey Rinpoche 2018.
6. See the last part of Khenchen Appey Rinpoche's commentary on the first line in this book for his explanation of Drakpa Gyaltsen's instructions.

7   The complete list of works given in the bibliography is based on research carried out by Rolf Scheuermann. See Scheuermann 2015.

8   These notes on Rinpoche's life are based on a brief chronological biography of Khenchen Appey Rinpoche published by Khenchen Sönam Gyatso in 2022 (mkhan chen bsod rnams rgya mtsho. 'jam mgon sa paN gnyis pa mkhan chen a pad rin po che'i rnam thar 'bring po deb ther dkar po. Rajpur, Dehradun: Sakya College, 2022.) For this brief presentation, the names of the texts Rinpoche received teachings on and transmitted to others were omitted. These details can be found in the Tibetan text. Details for the later periods of his life were added from biographies published with previous translations of Khenchen Appey Rinpoche's teachings.

9   Tib. 'jam dpal dgyes pa'i bshes gnyen tshangs sras bzhad pa'i blo gros.

10 These three texts represent the foundation for the study of tantra in the Sakya tradition: *An Overview of Tantra* (*rgyud sde spyi'i rnam*) by Sönam Tsemo, *The Great Tree of Realization* (*mngon rtogs ljon shing*) by Sönam Tsemo and Drakpa Gyaltsen, and the *Two Sections* (*rtag gnyis*) of the Hevajra Tantra, based on the commentaries by Drakpa Gyaltsen and Loter Wangpo.

A Key to the Profound Essential Points

1   The *Abhisamayālaṃkāra* teaches the eight sets of realization: three knowledges of three types of āryas (resultant omniscience of buddhas, path knowledge of bodhisattvas and above, and ground knowledge of śrāvakas and above), four stages of practice leading to buddhahood, and dharmakāya.

2   This refers specifically to chapters four and eleven of the *Sūtrālaṃkāra*.

3   This relates to four mistaken views taught in the first four chapters of the *Catuḥśataka*: regarding the impermanent as permanent, suffering as pleasurable, the impure as pure, and the selfless as self.

4   See Atiśa's *Lamp for the Path to Enlightenment*.

5   These are Potowa Rinchensel, Chengawa Tsultrim Bar, Puchungwa Zhönnu Gyaltsen.

Introductory Teachings

1. According to this system there are four broad categories of ārya beings: stream-enterer, once-returner, non-returner, and arhat. Each of these has two levels: approaching the attainment of each level and the resultant state. Those who approach the level of stream-entry are in the process of directly seeing the four noble truths for the first time. Once this process is completed, they abide in the fruition of stream entry and begin approaching the next attainment, once-returner. When they have eliminated all afflictions of the desire realm, they attain the level of non-returner, and when all afflictions of the three realms are abandoned, they attain the level of an arhat.

2. The twenty-five aspects of reality, or tattvas, is a doctrine of the ancient Sāṃkhya school of Indian philosophy. It upholds a dualistic worldview, dividing reality into inactive, pure consciousness (*puruṣa*) and active materiality (*prakṛti*), the latter evolving into the various elements of nature, including intelligence (*buddhi*), self-grasping (*ahaṃkāra*), mind (*manas*), and five sense faculties, five faculties of action, five subtle elements, and five great elements.

3. These instructions were originally given at the conclusion of one teaching session, in the middle of the explanations of Asaṅga's key instructions for taking refuge. Since they represent a subject in their own right, we have chosen to give them their own dedicated space within this written commentary.

4. These are the stūpa of Boudhanath, the stūpa of Swayambhu, both in the Kathmandu valley, and the stūpa in Namobuddha, located about 40 km southeast of the capital.

5. Skt. *cittotpāda*; Tib. *sems bskyed*. The full Sanskrit term is *bodhicittotpāda* (Tib. *byang chub tu sems bskyed pa*), or "the generation of the resolve to attain awakening." In the context of the Mahāyāna, this resolve is often simply referred to as bodhicitta, or "mind of awakening."

The First Line: "If You Are Attached to This Life, You Are Not a Dharma Practitioner."

1. In his commentary on *The Way of the Bodhisattva*, Khenchen Appey Rinpoche explains these eighteen conditions as follows: "There are eight situations or physical conditions which lack the freedom to practice the Dharma, and to be spared these is called *ease*. Four of these physical conditions are outside the human realm and four are within it. The four outside the human realm are being born: (1) in the hell realm, (2) in the hungry ghost realm, (3) in the animal realm, or (4) as a long-living god. Within the human realm, we might be born: (5) in an uncivilized country where the Buddha's teachings are unheard of and no one practices the Dharma, (6) with impaired faculties, (7) in a place devoid of a buddha—that is, a place where no buddha has appeared, or (8) as a person whose mind is distorted by wrong views. *Riches* refers to the ten favorable conditions that allow someone to practice the Dharma. They are: (1) taking birth as a human being, (2) taking birth in a central land—that is, a place where the Buddhadharma is available, (3) possessing sound sense faculties—that is, one can see, hear, and so forth, (4) not having committed grave negative actions such as the five deeds of immediate retribution, (5) having faith in the Dharma taught by the Buddha, (6) living in a world in which a buddha has appeared, (7) taught the Dharma, (8) where the teachings are still available, (9) where others also follow his teachings, and (10) where all the conditions conducive for practice are available."

2. Müchen Sempa Chenpo Könchok Gyaltsen famously compiled a vast collection of teachings on mind training, which was translated and published by Thubten Jinpa as *Mind Training: The Great Collection*. His commentary, entitled Supplement to the Oral Tradition, is included in this collection. The section on karma begins on p. 456.

3. See the section "General advice for practice in retreat" in the introduction.

4. That is, by contemplating our precious human life, death and impermanence, and the workings of karma.

The Second Line: "If You Are Attached to Saṃsāra, You Have No Renunciation."

1. Skt. *kalala*; Tib. *mer mer po*.
2. The wheel of becoming is held in the fangs and claws of Yama, the lord of death, illustrating the pervasive nature of impermanence.

The Third Line: "If You Are Attached to Your Own Self-Interest, You Have No Bodhicitta."

1. See *Ornament of Mahāyāna Sūtras* 18.29–30: The ten are: (1) those who have strong desire; (2) those who face great obstacles; (3) those oppressed by suffering; (4) those who commit negative deeds out of ignorance; (5) those whose spiritual potential is cut off; (6) those who hold mistaken views of non-Buddhist traditions, specifically the belief in the self; (7) those who are born in the realms of form and formlessness; (8) those who practice mistaken paths thinking they will lead to liberation; (9) those who follow the path of individual liberation, even though they could have entered the Mahāyāna; and (10) those who are on the Mahāyāna path, but who cannot practice properly due to their lack of merit and wisdom.
2. The six perfections and their opposing factors are: (1) generosity and stinginess; (2) ethical discipline and corrupt conduct; (3) patience and hatred; (4) diligence and laziness; (5) concentration and distraction; and (6) wisdom and wrong understanding.
3. The three remaining transgressions are: praising oneself and deprecating others due to desire for gain and respect; harming others and not accepting their apologies due to hatred; and rejecting the true Mahāyāna Dharma and propounding a made-up doctrine instead.
4. Details for the different levels of training can be learned from Sakya Paṇḍita's *Clarifying the Sages Intent*. See Jackson (2015) 406f.
5. *The Way of the Bodhisattva* 3.11.
6. *An Analysis of the Three Vows* (*sdom gsum rab dbye*) is one of the most influential works by Sakya Paṇḍita and discusses the vows of

individual liberation, bodhicitta, and secret mantra. See Rhoton 2002.

7   See Chapter 8 of *The Way of the Bodhisattva*.

8   See *The Way of the Bodhisattva* 8.130.

9   Wyl. *pha rol tu phyin pa*.

10 The Tibetan expression includes the noun *pha rol* ("farther shore") and the verb *phyin pa* ("gone"), indicating the methods that lead to this state of perfect transcendence.

11 Sometimes the giving of loving kindness is mentioned separately as a fourth type of generosity.

12 That is, the object, the subject, and the act of giving itself.

THE FOURTH LINE: "IF THERE IS GRASPING, IT IS NOT THE VIEW."

1   These instructions are included in Jamgön Kongtrul's *Treasury of Oral Instructions* (*gdams ngag mdzod*). See Gyurme Dorje 2021.

2   For Khenchen Appey Rinpoche's teachings on the perfections not explained in detail here, see Khenchen Appey Rinpoche's *Teachings on Sakya Pandita's Clarifying the Sage's Intent*, as well as his *Cultivating the Middle Way: Oral Instructions Based on Candrakīrti's Entering the Middle Way*.

3   The five supernatural abilities derived from mastery of meditative absorption are: (1) the ability to perform miraculous deeds, (2) the ability to know other peoples' minds, (3) the ability to hear unobstructed by distance, (4) the ability to know one's own past lives, and (5) the ability to know where beings are reborn. The supernatural ability to know the exhaustion of defilements is exclusive to ārya beings who, on top of mastering meditative concentration, have also attained profound insight into reality.

4   Tib. *mthong chos bde gnas kyi bsam gtan*.

5   This paragraph was originally taught in the context of the next section on physical posture. It was moved here due to its relevance to the prerequisites for meditation.

⁶ These are: paying homage, making offerings, confessing misdeeds, rejoicing in the positive deeds of all, requesting the Dharma, supplicating the awakened ones to remain, and dedicating all merit to the benefit of all beings.

⁷ The bases of totality are discussed by Asaṅga in his *Compendium of Abhidharma*. See Boin-Webb 2001:255f. The practice with the bases of totality—known as *kasiṇa* in the Pāli tradition—is extensively taught in the *Visuddhimagga* by Buddhaghosa.

⁸ Once the mind has attained unified concentration by overcoming the main hindrances, it can enter progressively subtle levels of concentration. The first four levels are associated with the form realm because familiarization with these levels can compound rebirth in this realm. The subsequent four levels are similarly associated with the formless realm. The first concentration is characterized by five factors: coarse applied thought, subtle investigation, joy, bliss, and one-pointedness. The second concentration is free of applied thought and investigation, and has joy, bliss, and one-pointedness. The third concentration is also free of joy and possesses bliss and one-pointedness; and the fourth concentration is free of bliss and is characterized by pure one-pointedness.

⁹ The Tibetan term is *dran pa* (Skt. *smṛti*), which is translated as "mindfulness" in most contexts.

¹⁰ Tib. *shes rab zhi rags gyi rnam pa can*.

¹¹ The peak of existence is the name of the highest level of existence within saṃsāra.

¹² See Ngorchen Könchok Lhundrup's *Ornament to Beautify the Three Appearances*, pp. 185.

¹³ That is, it must be motivated by bodhicitta, carried out with the right view—which is the practice of wisdom itself—and dedicated to the attainment of buddhahood for the benefit of all beings.

¹⁴ The two types of selflessness are the lack of a self in the individual and the lack of inherent identity in phenomena.

¹⁵ The eleventh type of form called "non-perceptible form" (*avijñaptirūpa, rnam par rig byed min pa'i gzugs*) is taught in the Sarvāstivāda Abhidharma and is related to their explanation of

karma. According to this system, a non-perceptible form is the link between the intention to perform an action and its execution through body or speech.

16 According to the Mahāyāna Abhidharma, there are fifty-one mental factors. The mental factors included in the skandha of formations number forty-nine when the factors of sensation and perception are counted separately as two of the five skandhas. They are termed concomitant because they share five features with the main consciousness they arise together with: object, aspect, sense faculty, time, and substance.

17 The category of non-concomitant formations is a special group of phenomena that are neither mental nor material. Since they have no material properties derived from the elements, they are not listed under the skandha of form. They are listed under the mental skandha of formations due to their resemblance to mind, insofar as both are formless.

18 When it is stated that cause and result are "different," the implication is that they are inherently different and thus unrelated phenomena.

19 At the end of his teachings, Khenchen Appey Rinpoche offered words of advice to the Tibetan students of monastic universities, or shedras. Even though these were not translated into other languages at the time of the event, we have included excerpts of this speech here since some of his remarks are nevertheless relevant for all followers of the Buddhadharma. The full speech will be published separately.

Glossary

ABHIDHARMA (Skt.), Tib. *chos mngon pa*.
A group of Buddhist scriptures and teachings presenting the various topics taught by the Buddha in a scholastic and systematic way. One of the three collections of the Buddha's teachings. See also *Tripiṭaka*.

AFFLICTED MIND (*kliṣṭamanas, nyon mongs pa can gyi yid*).
The afflicted mind is a subtle aspect of consciousness which focuses on the continuum of the all-base consciousness, apprehending it as the self. It is the seventh type of consciousness in the eight-consciousness model of the mind according to Yogācāra.

AFFLICTION (*kleśa, nyon mongs pa*).
A state of mind that causes unrest and obstructs the realization of ultimate reality. The six root afflictions are ignorance, desire, anger, pride, doubt, and wrong views. The Abhidharma teachings list a further twenty secondary afflictions.

AGGREGATES. See *skandha*.

AKANIṢṬHA (Skt.), Tib. *'og min*.
Literally, "beneath None." Name of the highest divine abode of the form realm and of the pure field of saṃbhogakāya buddhas.

ARHAT (Skt.), Tib. *dgra bcom pa.*

A person who has achieved the spiritual goal of liberation from the cycle of existence by eliminating all mental afflictions from their mindstream. The Sanskrit term literally means "worthy one," whereas the Tibetan term means "foe destroyer."

ĀRYA (Skt.), Tib. *'phags pa.*

Literally, "noble." An individual on the Buddhist path who has attained advanced levels of realization. In the context of the Śrāvakayāna: those who have attained insight into the four truths; Mahāyāna: those who have gained direct realization of ultimate reality.

ASAṄGA (4th century).

An Indian Buddhist master instrumental in the formation of the Yogācāra tradition. The elder brother of Vasubandhu, Asaṅga is regarded in the Tibetan tradition as the human medium of the bodhisattva Maitreya who transcribed his teachings known as the Five Dharmas of Maitreya. Asaṅga authored a number of important works such as the *Levels of the Practice of Yoga* (*Yogācārabhūmi*), the *Summary of the Mahāyāna* (*Mahāyānasaṃgraha*), and the *Compendium of Abhidharma* (*Abhidharmasamuccaya*).

ASURA (Skt.), Tib. *lha ma yin.*

A class of god-like beings, known to be in constant conflict with the gods (devas) due to their jealousy.

ATIŚA, Jowo Jé Palden (982–1054), aka Dipaṃkara Śrījñāna.

An Indian Buddhist master from Bengal instrumental in the revival of Buddhism in Tibet in the eleventh century after its repression by King Langdarma. Atiśa gained renown in Tibet for his teachings on the graded path to enlightenment and on mind training.

AVALOKITEŚVARA (Skt.), Tib. *spyan ras gzigs*.

A bodhisattva on the tenth bhūmi, embodiment of the compassion of the buddhas.

BARI LOTSĀWA (1040–1112), Rinchen Drak.

A renowned Tibetan translator who traveled to Nepal and India, instrumental in bringing many tantric teachings to Tibet. Bari Lotsāwa served as the second throne holder of Sakya, after Khön Könchok Gyalpo, and was a teacher of Sachen Kunga Nyingpo.

BASES OF TOTALITY (*kṛtsnāyatana, zad par gyi skye mched*).

Ten objects of meditative practice in which the practitioner perceives all phenomena as a single element or quality. For example, perceiving everything as the earth element, or as blue in color, etc.

BHĀVAVIVEKA (6th century).

An Indian Madhyamaka master and founder of the Svātantrika school, known for advocating independent logical arguments to establish emptiness. Author of the *Madhyamakahṛdayakārikā* and *Tarkajvālā*.

BHŪMI (Skt.), Tib. *sa*.

Literally, "ground." The name for the levels of realization traversed by a bodhisattva on the path to enlightenment. The first bhūmi, called *Utter Joy*, is attained with the initial insight into ultimate reality. This insight is then cultivated along the successive stages of enlightenment up to the tenth and final bodhisattva bhūmi, *Cloud of Dharma*. The attainment of perfect buddhahood, which is the final goal, is also referred to as the eleventh bhūmi.

BODHGAYA.

The name of the place where Buddha Śākyamuni attained enlightenment, located in the Indian state of Bihar.

BODHICITTA (Skt.), Tib. *byang chub kyi sems*.

Literally, "mind of awakening." Bodhicitta is of two types: relative and ultimate. Relative bodhicitta (*kun rdzob byang sems*) refers to the resolve to attain buddhahood for the sake of all beings and the practices motivated by this intention, whereas ultimate bodhicitta (*don dam pa'i byang sems*) refers to the realization of emptiness or ultimate reality.

BODHISATTVA (Skt.), Tib. *byang chub sems dpa'*.

The name given to an individual who has generated the resolve to attain the state of complete buddhahood for the sake of other beings and traverses the stages of the bodhisattva path.

BODHISATTVA VOWS.

The formal commitment made by an individual who is intent on attaining buddhahood for the sake of all beings. It entails the observance of a number of precepts to ensure a steady progress on the path.

BUDDHA (Skt.), Tib. *sangs rgyas*.

A person who has attained true and complete awakening, perfectly free of all obscurations and endowed with perfect wisdom, compassion, and the ability to help others. One of the Three Jewels or objects of refuge for Buddhists. Buddha literally means "awakened one."

BUDDHAGUHYA (7th century).

Indian Buddhist master, known his influential commentaries on the tantras.

BUDDHAHOOD.

The aim to be achieved in the Mahāyāna; the state of true and complete enlightenment obtained by the elimination of the two veils, i.e., the veil of mental afflictions and the cognitive veil.

BUDDHA REALM (*buddhakṣetra, sangs rgyas kyi zhing*).

A domain or field that constitutes a particular buddha's sphere of influence and activity. These can be classified as pure realms (like Amitābha's Sukhāvatī) or impure realms (like our world system). Each realm manifests according to the specific aspirations of its presiding buddha.

BUTÖN (1290–1364), Rinchen Drup.

Renowned Tibetan scholar and historian who compiled and organized the Tibetan Buddhist canon, and served as abbot of Zhalu monastery.

CAKRASAṂVARA (Skt), Tib. *bde mchog 'khor lo*.

One of the principal deities and tantric systems in Vajrayāna Buddhism. Its practice is particularly important in the Sarma (new translation) schools of Tibetan Buddhism.

CALM ABIDING (*śamatha, zhi gnas*).

The name for meditation practice aimed at developing stability and clarity of mind. Paired with special insight, it becomes a powerful tool to uproot ignorance, the root cause of suffering.

CANDRAKĪRTI (fl. 7th century).

An Indian Buddhist master famous for his writings on Madhyamaka, most notably his *Entering the Middle Way* (*Madhyamakāvatāra*) and *Clear Words* (*Prasannapadā*).

CHEKAWA YESHÉ DORJÉ (1101–1175).

A Tibetan Kadampa master and compiler of the *Mind Training in Seven Points*. He was instrumental in the propagation of teachings on lojong (mind training) in Tibet, which he himself had received from Geshe Sharawa.

Chögyal Phagpa (1235–1280).

The fifth of the five founding masters of the Sakya tradition and the nephew of Sakya Paṇḍita. He accompanied his uncle to live at the Mongol court, where he later functioned as the imperial preceptor of the Yuan dynasty, holding both spiritual and worldly authority over Tibet.

Chogye Trichen Rinpoche (1919–2007).

An eminent Sakya master who held the Tsarpa lineage of the Sakya tradition. He was renowned for his mastery of both sūtra and tantra, and his profound accomplishment; he served as a teacher to many high lamas including the 14th Dalai Lama.

Cittamātra (Skt.), Tib. *sems tsam*.

Literally, "mind only." A Mahāyāna school of thought known as Vijñānavāda ('Consciousness school') or Vijñaptimātra ('Cognition-Only'). The Cittamātra school is related to the Yogācāra tradition founded by the Indian masters Asaṅga and Vasubandhu and is based on the sūtras of the third turning of the Dharma wheel and the teachings of the Bodhisattva Maitreya. The unique approach of this school consists in aiming to demonstrate that everything in the world is nothing but mind, in other words that the objects one relates to are nothing but mental representations devoid of external independent existence. The mind freed of this falsely imagined duality of subject and object is thus liberated from the ignorance at the root of all suffering.

Conditioning factors (*saṃskāra, 'du byed*).

The name of the fourth skandha, also called "formations" or "formative factors." It is an umbrella term covering the mental factors that condition perception and generate karma.

CONVENTIONAL REALITY. See *two realities*.

DEPENDENT ARISING (*pratītyasamutpāda*, *rten cing 'brel bar 'byung ba*).

The process of conditioned existence bringing about rebirth and suffering. The twelve links of dependent arising are ignorance, karmic formations, consciousness, name and form, sense bases, contact, sensation, craving, clinging, becoming, birth, and aging and death.

DEZHUNG CHOKTRUL RINPOCHE (1885–1952), Dezhung Anjam Kunga Tenpé Gyaltsen.

A recent Sakya master from Dezhung, East Tibet, Dezhung Anjam Rinpoche was a disciple of Jamyang Khyentse Chökyi Lodro and Gatön Ngawang Lekpa, and one of the root gurus of Khenchen Appey Rinpoche.

DHARMA (Skt.), Tib. *chos*.

When capitalized, this term refers to the Buddha's teachings and the path of practice and experience based on them. It is one of the Three Jewels or objects of refuge for Buddhists. In general, however, the term *dharma* has more than ten different meanings, including *phenomenon* and *religious tradition*.

DHARMAKĀYA. See *kāya*.

DHARMAKĪRTI (7th century).

Indian Buddhist master celebrated for his seven works on logic and epistemology in the tradition of the great master Dignāga. His most important treatise is the *Commentary on the Means of Valid Cognition* (*Pramāṇavārttika*).

DRAKPA GYALTSEN (1147–1216), Jetsün Rinpoche Drakpa Gyaltsen.
The third of the five founding masters of the Sakya tradition. He was one of the sons of Sachen Kunga Nyingpo and the uncle and root guru of Sakya Paṇḍita.

DZONGSAR MONASTERY.
Sakya monastery in East Tibet, Degé county, established in the 13th century by Chögyal Phagpa.

EMPOWERMENT (*abhiṣeka, dbang bskur*).
A ritual carried out by a qualified Vajrayāna master that enables the disciple to enter the path of Secret Mantra.

EMPTINESS (*śūnyatā, stong pa nyid*).
A name for ultimate reality. It refers to the fact that since phenomena arise depending on causes and conditions, they lack an inherent substantial nature of their own. The insight into this reality functions as the gateway to the freedom from conceptual proliferations, which are at the root of karma and the afflictions.

ETHICAL DISCIPLINE (*śīla, tshul khrims*).
One of the three higher trainings comprising the Buddhist path. Also one of the six pāramitās. In the Mahāyāna, discipline entails abandoning harmful conduct, engaging in wholesome deeds, and benefitting others. See also *pāramitā*.

FIVE SKANDHAS. See *skandhas*.

FIVE PATHS (*pañca mārga, lam lnga*).
The five stages of the path to awakening: the path of accumulation, the path of joining, the path of seeing, the path of cultivation, and the path of no further training. See individual entries for each path.

FOUR NOBLE TRUTHS (*āryasatya, 'phags pa'i bden pa bzhi*).

The foundational teaching of the Buddha forming the framework for understanding both cyclic existence and liberation. The four truths are the truth of suffering, the truth of the origin of suffering, the truth of the cessation of suffering, and the truth of the path leading to cessation. These truths follow a medical model: identifying the disease, its cause, the possibility of cure, and the treatment.

FOUR POWERS (Tib. *stobs bzhi*).

Four essential qualites in the practice of confession and purification: the power of remorse, the power of support, the power of remedial action, and the power of resolve.

FOUR SEALS OF THE BUDDHIST VIEW.

Four fundamental principles that define the understanding of reality according to the Buddha's teaching: (1) all compounded phenomena are impermanent; (2) all defiled states are suffering; (3) all phenomena are empty and selfless, and (4) nirvāṇa is peace.

GELUK (Tib. *dge lugs*).

Literally, "way of virtue." The youngest of the four main traditions of Buddhism established in Tibet, also known as the Ganden School. This tradition follows the teachings of Lama Tsongkhapa Lobsang Dragpa (1357–1419). It is particularly renowned for its emphasis on monastic training and its rigorous scholastic education.

GORAMPA SÖNAM SENGE (1429–1490), Künkhyen Gorampa.

A Sakya master from East Tibet whose writings, especially his philosophical works, have become classic reference works for scholars of later generations.

GRASPING (Tib. *'dzin pa*).

The cognitive process of apprehending an object of perception. In the context of Buddhist philosophy, "grasping" specifically refers to the act of apprehending associated with an erroneous belief about the nature of the object, be it its existence, nonexistence, both, or neither.

GUGÉ.

An ancient kingdom in Western Tibet that played a crucial role in the second dissemination of Buddhism in Tibet. It was an important center of Buddhist learning and translation from the 10th to 17th centuries.

GYALSÉ NGULCHU TOKMÉ ZANGPO (1297–1371).

A very learned and accomplished Kadampa master, famous for his teachings on bodhicitta. His most widely studied texts are *The Thirty-Seven Practices of the Bodhisattvas* and his commentary on the *Way of the Bodhisattva* by Śāntideva.

HEVAJRA (Skt.), Tib. *kye rdo rje*.

A principal meditational deity and tantric system particularly important in the Sakya tradition.

HIGHER REALMS (*svarga, mtho ris*).

The three types of existence in saṃsāra characterised by less obvious forms of suffering than in the lower realms, and by the possibility of attaining liberation. They are the human realm, the realm of demi-gods, and the realm of divine beings.

HIGHER TRAININGS, THREE.

The essence of the Buddhist path, consisting of the trainings in discipline (*śīla, tshul khrims*), meditative concentration (*samādhi, ting nge 'dzin*) and wisdom (*prajñā, shes rab*).

HĪNAYĀNA (Skt.), Lesser Vehicle (Tib. *theg dman*).

The foundational Buddhist system of theory and practice based on the first turning of the Dharma wheel (i.e., the teaching of the four ārya truths). It is also defined as the path of individual liberation, emphasizing renunciation and taken by individuals of lesser abilities who are concerned mainly with their own liberation from suffering. This path can thus be defined on the basis of the philosophical system adhered to (i.e., either Vaibhāṣika, based on the tenets exposed in the *Mahāvibhāṣa* Abhidharma treatise; or Sautrāntika, based on tenets exposed in the sūtras), or the motivation of the practitioner (in which case it should not be conflated with the Theravada path, which may be practiced with the motivation to attain buddhahood for the sake of all beings).

IGNORANCE (*avidyā, ma rig pa*).

In the Buddhist context, ignorance refers to a misunderstanding of reality, not a mere lack of knowledge. Ignorance occurs on many levels and can be explained in numerous ways. One way is to distinguish three types of ignorance: (1) the ignorance that is one of the three mental poisons (desire, hatred, and ignorance); (2) the ignorance that is the first of the twelve links of dependent arising; and (3) the ignorance that is the root of the twelve links. Ignorance in terms of the three poisons is an incorrect understanding of the principle of karma, cause and effect, and thus leads to the accumulation of the causes of suffering. The ignorance that is the first of the twelve links is a misapprehension of reality in terms of apprehending a self in the individual. The ignorance that is the root of the twelve links is a misapprehension of reality in terms of apprehending inherent identity in phenomena. The latter is the most fundamental form of ignorance, giving rise to all other aspects of confusion.

INDIVIDUAL (*pudgala, gang zag*).

The individual person or being in any of the six realms of existence. The individual is composed of various skandhas or constituent factors, comprising a physical form (which ranges from gross forms that can be directly perceived to imperceptible, extremely subtle ones, such as in the case of beings in the so-called "formless" realm), consciousness, and mental factors. Even though there is no permanent, singular, and independent identity or self to be found among these factors, the concept of "I" is generated on the basis of a misapprehension of the skandhas.

INHERENT IDENTITY. See *self*.

JAMBUDVĪPA (Skt.), Tib. *'dzam bu gling*.

Literally, "Rose Apple Continent." The southern continent according to ancient Indian cosmology and the world of humans. It can also refer to the Indian subcontinent.

JAMGÖN KONGTRUL (1813–1899), Lodrö Tayé.

A prominent Kagyu master from Degé, East Tibet, known for his scholarship and the compilation of the Five Great Treasuries. He collaborated closely with Jamyang Khyentse Wangpo in preserving the teachings of all traditions.

JAMYANG KHYENTSE CHÖKYI LODRÖ (1893–1959).

A preeminent master of the 20th century who was recognized as an incarnation of Jamyang Khyentse Wangpo. He was instrumental in preserving many rare lineages and teachings during the critical period of Tibet's transition.

JAMYANG KHYENTSE WANGPO (1820–1892).

A prominent Sakya master from Degé, East Tibet, and key figure of the non-sectarian (*rimé*) activities that significantly influenced Tibetan Buddhism. Known as a true polymath and treasure revealer, he is renowned for preserving and transmitting a vast amount of teachings from all Buddhist traditions, many of which were in danger of being lost.

JONANG (Tib. *jo nang*).

A school of Tibetan Buddhism known for its teachings on shentong ("empty of other") philosophy and Kālacakra practice.

KADAMPA (Tib. *bka' gdams pa*).

Literally, "words and instructions." One of the earliest schools of Tibetan Buddhism established during the second dissemination of the Dharma. The tradition was founded by disciples of Dromtönpa (1005–1064), who was himself a student of Atiśa. The emphasis in the Kadam tradition is on the practice of mind training (Tib. *blo sbyong*) and on the secrecy of tantric practice. Although it vanished as an independent school a long time ago, its teachings are preserved and cherished by all Tibetan traditions.

KAGYÜ (Tib. *bka' brgyud*).

Literally, "oral lineage." One of the major schools of Tibetan Buddhism, also known as the Practice Lineage (Tib. *grub brgyud*), established during the period of the second dissemination of the Dharma in Tibet. The teachings of this tradition go back to the translator Marpa (1012–1097), his foremost disciple, the celebrated yogin Milarepa (1040–1123), and the latter's student Gampopa (1079–1173). The school is famous for its Mahāmudrā ('Great Seal') teachings on the nature of mind, and its yogic practices including the Six Yogas of Nāropa.

KAMALAŚĪLA (740–795 CE).

Indian Buddhist master and key figure in the history Tibetan Buddhism, Kamalaśīla famously defended the position of a gradual approach to enlightenment at the Great Debate of

Samyé held in Tibet, against his Chinese rival who argued for an instantenous approach. He was also an influential author, whose writings include three *Bhāvanākrama* texts on the stages of meditation.

KANGYUR (Tib. *bka' 'gyur*).
Literally, "translations of the words." The central component of the Tibetan Buddhist canon, containing the translations of the words of the Buddha, including both sūtras and tantras.

KARMA (Skt.), Tib. *las*.
Literally, "action." The natural law of actions and their results. According to the Buddha's teaching, it is mainly the intention behind an action which determines whether it is wholesome, unwholesome, or neutral.

KĀYA (Skt.), Tib. *sku*.
Literally, "body." A buddha's awakening has three levels of manifestation, called the *three kāyas*. These are (1) the *dharmakāya* or 'dharma-body' (*chos sku*), which is a buddha's perfect realization of ultimate reality and is not perceptible to others; (2) the *saṃbhogakāya* or 'body of enjoyment' (*longs sku*) – the pure manifestation of this realization in forms perceptible to bodhisattvas on the highest level of realization; and (3) the *nirmāṇakāya* or 'emanation body' (*sprul sku*) – the manifestation of enlightenment accessible to ordinary beings. Sometimes a fourth kāya is added: the *svabhāvikakāya* or 'essence body' (Tib. *ngo bo nyid kyi sku*), which refers to the inseparability of the three kāyas.

KHENPO (Tib. *mkhan po*).
Monastic title for a qualified preceptor.

KHÖN (Tib. *'khon*).

One of the most important ancestral clans in Tibetan Buddhist history, the Khön family lineage became the hereditary holders of the Sakya throne.

KHÖN GYICHU DRALHAWAR (11th century).

A paternal relative and teacher of Sachen Kunga Nyingpo who transmitted to him the Hevajra teachings coming from Drokmi Lotsāwa.

KHÖN KÖNCHOK GYALPO (1034–1102).

The founder of Sakya Monastery established in 1073, disciple of Drokmi Lotsāwa, and the father of Sachen Kunga Nyingpo.

KHÖN LUI WANGPO (8th century).

An ancestor of the Khön family who was among the first seven Tibetans to be ordained as Buddhist monks during the time of King Trisong Detsen and one of the twenty-five principal disciples of Padmasambhava.

KUNGA DROLCHOK (1507–1566).

A master from Mustang known for his non-sectarian approach and preservation of various Buddhist lineages. Originally affiliated with the Sakya tradition, Kunga Drolchok had deep ties with the Shangpa Kagyu and Jonang traditions, and served as the twenty-fourth abbot of Jonang Monastery.

LAMA (Tib. *bla ma*).

The Tibetan term for *guru*, meaning spiritual guide or teacher.

LAMDRÉ (Tib. *lam 'bras*)

Literally, "path and result." A cycle of teachings unique to the Sakya tradition. The Lamdré teachings are based on the Hevajra Tantra and originated with the Indian adept Mahasiddha Virupa. They comprise the entire range of

Buddhist teachings, from sūtra to tantra. Two Lamdré traditions exist today: Lobshé ("explanations for disciples") and Tsokshé ("explanations for the assembly").

LAMRIM (Tib. *lam rim*).
Literally, "stages of the path." The name of a Tibetan Buddhist literary genre popular in the Geluk tradition and going back to the teachings of Atiśa. Lamrim represents a systematic and gradual approach to the path to enlightenment, including theory and practice.

LANGDARMA (r. 838–842)
The 42nd and last king of the Tibetan Empire, infamous for his persecution of Buddhism in Tibet. His reign marked the end of Tibet's imperial period and led to the fragmentation of the Tibetan empire.

LIBERATION (*mokṣa, thar pa*).
The state of freedom from suffering and its causes, that is, karma and afflictions.

LOJONG (Tib. *blo sbyong*).
Literally, "mind training." The name for Mahāyāna methods of mind training based on the practice of bodhicitta.

LOWER REALMS (*durgati, ngan song*).
The three types of existence in saṃsāra characterized by great suffering, namely the animal realm, the realm of hungry ghosts, and the hell realm.

LUMINOSITY (*prabhāsvara, 'od gsal*).
The mind's most subtle, inherent cognitive ability, obscured by afflictions and conceptual thought.

MĀLĀ (Skt.).
The garland of beads used to count mantras, typically 108 beads.

MADHYAMAKA (Skt.), Tib. *dbu ma*.

Literally, "middle way." A Mahāyāna school of thought and practice founded by the Indian master Nāgārjuna, based on the sūtras of the second turning of the Dharma wheel. This approach emphasizes the lack of any substantial nature in phenomena, based on the doctrine of dependent origination. It is called the Middle Way because its practice frees the mind of the conceptual extremes of both existence and nonexistence. In the Tibetan tradition, this school is generally held to represent the supreme philosophical view.

MAHĀSIDDHA VIRŪPA (8th–9th century).

One for the eighty-four Indian mahāsiddhas, or accomplished tantric adepts, and author of the *Vajra Verses*, which are the source of the Lamdré teachings.

MAHĀYĀNA (Skt.), Tib. *theg pa chen po*.

Literally, "great vehicle." The system of Buddhist theory and practice based on the second and third turnings of the Dharma wheel (i.e., the profound teachings on emptiness and the teachings on the discrimination between the definitive and the provisional teachings). This vehicle is also termed the bodhisattva path, taken by those motivated by great compassion and the wish to attain buddhahood for the sake of all beings.

MAITREYA (Skt.), Tib. *byams pa mgon po*.

A bodhisattva on the tenth bhūmi and the future buddha, currently residing in the heavenly realm of Tuṣita. Maitreya transmitted five teachings to his human disciple Asaṅga which are known as the *Five Dharmas of Maitreya*: *Ornament of Realization* (*Abhisamayālaṁkāra*), *Ornament of the Mahāyāna Sūtras* (*Mahāyānasūtrālaṁkāra*), *Treatise on the Sublime Continuum of the Mahāyāna*

(*Mahāyānottaratantraśāstra*), *Distinguishing the Middle from the Extremes* (*Madhyāntavibhāga*), and *Distinguishing Dharmas from Their True Nature* (*Dharmadharmatāvibhāga*).

MAL LOTSĀWA LODRÖ DRAKPA (11th century).

A significant translator and teacher of Sachen Kunga Nyingpo, to whom he transmitted many teachings, in particular the Dharma cycles on Cakrasaṃvara, Vajrayoginī, and Dharma protectors.

MAṆḌALA OFFERING.

A ritual offering of the entire universe visualized as a pure land.

MAÑJUŚRĪ (Skt.), Tib. *'jam dpal*.

A bodhisattva on the tenth bhūmi, embodiment of the wisdom of the buddhas.

MĀRA (Skt.), Tib. *bdud*.

In the Buddhist context this term refers to the forces obstructing awakening. The tradition speaks of four māras: the māra of the aggregates, the māra of mental afflictions, the māra of the lord of death, and the māra of the child of gods.

MIND TRAINING. See *lojong*.

MÜCHEN SEMPA CHENPO KÖNCHOK GYALTSEN (1388–1469).

A disciple of the Sakya masters Rongtön Sheja Künrig (1367–1449) and Ngorchen Kunga Zangpo (1382–1456), and second abbot of Ngor monastery. Together with Sempa Chenpo Zhönnu Gyaltsen, Müchen compiled the mind training collection *Hundred Instructions on Mind Training* (*blo sbyong brgya rtsa*).

NĀGA (Skt.), Tib. *klu*.

Serpent being believed to inhabit subterranean and watery areas. While certain nāgas are powerful, benevolent protectors of the Dharma, others can be malicious and cause diseases.

NĀGĀRJUNA (1st century CE).

A South Indian Buddhist master and founder of the Madhyamaka tradition, famous for his collection of philosophical treatises, among which figures his *Verses on the Root Middle Way* (*Mūlamadhyamakakārikā*), and his collection of devotional works.

NGORCHEN KÖNCHOK LHUNDRUP (1497–1557).

The tenth abbot of Ngor monastery and an important commentator on the Lamdré teachings.

NGORCHEN KUNGA ZANGPO (1382–1456).

A Sakya master and the founder and first abbot of Ngor Evam Chöden monastery in central Tibet.

NGOR MONASTERY, Ngor Evam Chöden.

A Sakya monastery in central Tibet founded in the 15th century by Ngorchen Kunga Zangpo. Ngor Evam Chöden is the second most important seat of the Sakya tradition and an important center of tantric studies and for the monastic lineage.

NIRMĀṆAKĀYA. See *kāya*.

NIRVĀṆA (Skt.), Tib. *mya ngan las 'das pa*.

The Tibetan term literally means "state beyond sorrow." The general name for the purpose of the Buddhist path, equivalent to liberation from saṃsāra. Two types of nirvāṇa are distinguished: the nirvāṇa of the Hīnayāna, which is the individual's liberation from saṃsāra resulting from the cessation of afflictions and their causes, and the nirvāṇa of the Mahāyāna, also called "nonabiding nirvāṇa," which refers to a state beyond both ordinary existence and cessation.

NON-PERCEPTIBLE FORM (*avijñaptirūpa, rnam par rig byed min pa'i gzugs*).

A type of form taught in the Sarvāstivāda Abhidharma related to their explanation of karma. According to this system, a non-perceptible form is the link between the intention to perform an action and its execution through body or speech.

NON-RETURNER (*anāgāmī, phyir mi 'ong pa*).

The third of four levels of realization on the śrāvaka path, attained when all afflictions of the desire realm have been eliminated. This stage ensures no further rebirth in the desire realm. From that moment onward, if further lives are required to eliminate any remaining afflictions, rebirth can only occur in the pure abodes of the form realm.

NO-SELF. See *selflessness*.

ONCE-RETURNER (*sakṛdāgāmī, lan cig phyir 'ong ba*).

The second of four levels of realization on the śrāvaka path, attained when most afflictions of the desire realm have been eliminated and only one more human birth is required to eliminate the remaining ones.

PADMASAMBHAVA (8th century), Guru Rinpoche.

The "Lotus-Born" master from Oḍḍiyāna who, together with the abbot Śāntarakṣita, played a crucial role in establishing Buddhism in Tibet during the reign of King Trisong Detsen. Revered in Tibet as the second Buddha, he famously subdued local spirits and established the first monastery at Samyé.

PĀRAMITĀ (Skt.), Tib. *pha rol tu phyin pa*.

Literally, "perfection." The name for the practices a bodhisattva engages in to attain buddhahood. They are the pāramitās of generosity, discipline, forbearance, diligence, concentration, and wisdom. To this list are sometimes added the pāramitās of skillful means, aspiration, power, and gnosis.

PĀRAMITĀYĀNA (Skt.), Tib. *phar phyin theg pa*.

Literally, "perfection vehicle." Following the Mahāyāna, two pathways lead to complete awakening, or buddhahood: the Pāramitā Vehicle and the Secret Mantra Vehicle, or Vajrayāna. On the Pāramitā Vehicle one will mainly practice the pāramitās, whereas a practitioner of the Secret Mantra Vehicle will make use of the skillful means taught in the tantras.

PARINIRVĀṆA (Skt.), Tib. *yongs su myang 'das*.

The final nirvāṇa of an enlightened being attained upon the perishing of the physical body.

PATH OF ACCUMULATION (*saṃbhāra mārga, tshogs lam*).

The first of the five stages of the path to awakening, attained upon generating bodhicitta out of great compassion for sentient beings. The practice at this stage consists of gathering the accumulations of merit by means of altruistically motivated deeds, and of wisdom, mainly based on study and contemplation.

PATH OF CULTIVATION (*bhāvanā mārga, sgom lam*).

The fourth of the five stages of the path to awakening. After seeing emptiness directly for the first time in the previous stage (i.e., path of seeing), this path consists of deepening the realization by cultivating in meditation the newly gained insight and of gathering powerful merit dedicated to the attainment of buddhahood. In this way, one gradually removes the cognitive veils, thereby attaining increasingly higher levels of realization, i.e., the second to the tenth bodhisattva grounds.

PATH OF JOINING (*prayoga mārga, sbyor lam*).

The second of the five stages of the path to awakening. At this stage one mainly engages in meditation on emptiness based on the understanding gained on the previous stage. This path is divided into four levels, which represent increasingly higher levels of realization: heat (one starts to feel the 'heat' of the 'fire of emptiness', which burns away all afflictions); peak (the realization reaches a new summit on which the roots of goodness become indestructible); forbearance (one is able to fearlessly forbear the reality of emptiness); and supreme dharma (the last phase of worldly existence, immediately preceding the direct realization of emptiness). This path is called "path of joining", because it functions as a link, bringing the mind to the realization of emptiness.

PATH OF NO FURTHER TRAINING (*aśaikṣa mārga, mi slob lam*).

The fifth and last of the five stages of the path to awakening. Having completely eliminated both veils, one attains the stage of buddhahood, consisting of the three kāyas of perfect awakening.

PATH OF SEEING (*darśana mārga, mthong lam*).

The third of the five stages of the path to awakening. This path consists of the direct, non-conceptual realization of emptiness. At this stage, the veil of afflictions is eliminated and one reaches the first bodhisattva bhūmi, thus becoming an ārya being.

PERFECTION OF WISDOM (*prajñāpāramitā, shes rab kyi pha rol tu phyin pa*).

The highest insight into ultimate reality according to the Mahāyāna, and the name of an extensive corpus of sūtras and related literature teaching this wisdom.

PERFECTIONS, six. See *pāramitā*.

PLIANCY (*praśrabdhi*, *shin sbyangs*).

In the context of meditation training, pliancy is the quality of a well-trained mind, free of hindrances, flexible, and fit to the task.

PRATYEKABUDDHA (Skt.), solitary realizer (Tib. *rang sangs rgyas*).

An individual on the Hīnayāna path of individual liberation who practices the Dharma during periods when no teachings of a buddha are available. Pratyekabuddhas live in solitude or in groups and, without relying on a teacher, become realized through their insight into the principle of dependent arising.

RONGTÖN SHEJA KUNRIG (1367–1449).

A prominent Sakya master renowned for his scholarship, particularly in Madhyamaka philosophy and the treatises of Maitreya. He founded Penpo Nalendra Monastery in central Tibet and his teachings significantly influenced the development of Tibetan Buddhism.

RŪPAKĀYA (Skt.), Tib. *gzugs sku*.

Literally, "form body." The umbrella term for the two types of forms manifested by a fully awakened buddha to benefit others, i.e., *saṃbhogakāya*, or body of enjoyment, and *nirmāṇakāya*, or emanation body. See *kāya*.

SACHEN KUNGA NYINGPO (1092–1158).

The first of the five founding masters of the Sakya tradition and the son of Khön Könchok Gyalpo, who established the seat of the Sakya tradition.

SĀDHANA (Skt.), Tib. *grub thabs*.

Literally, "means of accomplishment." The name for tantric practice liturgies, involving visualization of deities, making offerings and praises, usually mantra recitation, and other practices.

SAKYA (Tib. *sa skya*).

Literally, "grey earth." One of the major schools of Tibetan Buddhism, established during the period of the second dissemination of the Dharma in Tibet, and named after the place in southern Tibet where its principal monastery was founded in 1073. The five founding masters of this tradition were Sachen Kunga Nyingpo (1092–1158), Sönam Tsemo (1142–1182), Dragpa Gyaltsen (1147–1216), Sakya Paṇḍita (1182–1251), and Chögyal Phagpa (1235–1280). This school is famous for its extensive philosophical training and as the upholder of the Lamdré teachings originating with the Indian master Virūpa.

SAKYA PAṆḌITA (1182–1251), Kunga Gyaltsen.

One of the founding masters of the Sakya school. Sakya Paṇḍita was famous for his strict adherence to the Indian traditions of Buddhism, for his very extensive knowledge of all the classical Indian fields of knowledge, and particularly for his writings on epistemology. He travelled to China to serve as the main spiritual teacher at the Mongol court.

SAMĀDHI (Skt.), Tib. *ting nge 'dzin*.

A general term used to denote deep levels of meditative concentration. The practice of samādhi constitutes one of the three pillars of Buddhist practice, the other two being ethical discipline and wisdom.

ŚAMATHA. See *calm abiding*.

SAMBHOGAKĀYA. See *kāya*.

SAMSĀRA (Skt.), Tib. *'khor ba*.

The beginningless and ceaselessly repetitive cycle of uncontrolled birth and death which beings are subject to as long as they are not enlightened. This perpetual cycle of worldly existence is characterized by unsatisfactoriness and a lack of true freedom.

SANGHA (Skt.), Tib. *dge 'dun.*

The community of those practicing the Buddha's path. In the Mahāyāna, this term refers in particular to realized bodhisattvas. It is the third object of refuge, one of the Three Jewels.

ŚĀNTARAKṢITA (725–788).

The Indian Buddhist master and abbot of the Buddhist university of Nālandā who, together with Padmasambhava, helped establish Buddhism in Tibet during the reign of King Trisong Detsen. He ordained the first Tibetan monks and established the monastic system in Tibet.

ŚĀNTIDEVA (8th century).

Indian Buddhist master and proponent of the Madhyamaka tradition who taught at Nālanda University; author of the celebrated *The Way of the Bodhisattva (Bodhicaryāvatāra)*.

ŚĀRIPUTRA.

One of the two chief disciples of the Buddha, alongside Maudgalyāyana, Śāriputra is renowned for his exceptional wisdom.

SARVĀSTIVĀDA (Skt.), Tib. *thams cad yod par smra ba.*

Literally, "proponents of 'all exists'." School of early Buddhism, listed among the eighteen schools of the Hīnayāna and origin of the Vaibhāṣika and Sautrāntika schools. Known as an Abhidharma tradition, one of the principal tenets of Sarvāstivāda is that dharmas, i.e., the constituent elements of reality, have permanent existence throughout past, present, and future.

ŚĀSTRA (Skt.), Tib. *bstan bcos*.
Authoritative treatises composed by Indian masters based on the sūtras.

SAUTRĀNTIKA (Skt.), Tib. *mdo sde pa*.
Literally, "sūtra follower." One of the two subschools of the Hīnayāna, so called due to its adherence to the words of the Buddha as recorded in the sūtras and, as opposed the Vaibhāṣika school, its rejection of the authority of the Abhidharma.

SECRET MANTRAYĀNA (*guhyamantrayāna, gsang sngags kyi theg pa*).
The tantric path of Mahāyāna Buddhism, also called Vajrayāna, based on a specific class of scriptures called tantras, and characterized by the great number of skillful means used to attain enlightenment. This name emphasizes the use of mantras and the secret nature of this path, being revealed only to those who have received the appropriate empowerments and subsequent permissions. See also *Vajrayāna*.

SELF (*ātman, bdag*).
An inherent identity attributed to phenomena. Two types of self are distinguished: a self in the individual (*pudgalātman, gang zag gi bdag*) and an inherent identity in phenomena (*dharmātman, chos kyi bdag*). The *self in the individual* is a mistaken notion apprehending an inherent identity on the basis of the five skandhas. The direct realization that the five skandhas are devoid of a self is the liberating insight that frees from saṃsāra, tantamount to the attainment of arhatship. The *inherent identity in phenomena* is a more subtle mistaken notion based on the misapprehension of the individual phenomena comprising the skandhas, as well as all other

objects of perception. The complete realization of the lack of inherent identity of all phenomena is achieved only by a fully awakened buddha.

SELF-GRASPING (*ātmagrāha, bdag 'dzin*).
The thought "I" that arises in dependence on an individual's body, the sensations they experience, and their mind. The belief in the true existence of the self.

SELFLESSNESS (*anātman, bdag med*).
The lack of true existence of a self.

SERLINGPA (10th century).
Renowned master from the "golden island" of Sumatra, Serlingpa was the main teacher of Atiśa, who travelled to study lojong mind training under him for twelve years.

SEVEN-LIMB LITURGY, seven-limb practice.
A practice involving seven steps that function as a preliminary purification for the main practice: prostration, offerings, confession, rejoicing, requesting the buddhas to teach, and supplicating them not to enter nirvāṇa.

SHEDRA (Tib. *bshad grwa*)
Department within a Tibetan monastery specialized in the study of philosphical texts.

SKANDHA (Skt.), Tib. *phung po.*
Literally, "heap." The psycho-physical constituents of a sentient being, often called "aggregates." Five skandhas characterize human experience: one group of physical phenomena (i.e., the skandha of form) and four groups of mental phenomena (sensations, perceptions, formations, and consciousness). The notion of self is superimposed on the basis of the five skandhas.

SONGTSEN GAMPO (r. 617–650).

The first of the three Dharma Kings of Tibet who unified the Tibetan plateau and initiated the first transmission of Buddhism to Tibet. He is credited with building the first Buddhist temples in Tibet, most notably the Jokhang temple in Lhasa.

SPECIAL INSIGHT (*vipaśyanā, lhag mthong*).

The cultivation of insight into the true nature of reality in order to eliminate mental afflictions and the suffering they produce. One of the two main branches of Buddhist meditation, the practice of special insight must be based on a mind trained in calm abiding—the other branch—in order to function as a liberating method.

ŚRĀVAKA (Skt.), Tib. *nyan thos*.

Literally, "hearer." The disciples of Buddha Śākyamuni who practice the teachings of the Lesser Vehicle. The Sanskrit term śrāvaka comes from the two words *śruta* (hearing) and *vāk* (speech), meaning that they listened and then spoke to others what they had heard.

ŚRĀVAKAYĀNA (Skt.), Tib. *nyan thos theg pa*.

Literally, "hearer vehicle." The path of those following the Hīnayāna approach leading to the attainment of arhat.

STREAM-ENTERER (*śrotāpanna, rgyun zhugs*).

The first of four levels of realization on the śrāvaka path, attained through insight into the four noble truths.

STŪPA (Skt.), Tib. *mchod rten*.

A dome-shaped Buddhist monument used to house sacred relics or commemorate significant sites.

GLOSSARY — 231

SUBTLE CHANNELS (*nāḍi, rtsa*).

The pathways for the energy winds and bindus in the subtle body.

SŪTRA (Skt.), Tib. *mdo*.

Scriptures believed to contain the actual words of the Buddha, revealing his exoteric teachings for the general public. The sūtras have been commented on in the *śāstras* or commentarial treatises, and their essential points for practice have been extracted in the *upadeśa* texts or pith instructions. Also, one of the three collections of the Buddha's teachings. See *Tripiṭaka*.

SŪTRA TRADITION.

The tradition of the Mahāyāna or Great Vehicle that follows the teachings expounded in the sūtras, rather than in the tantras. See *sūtra, tantra*.

TAKTSANG LOTSĀWA SHERAB RINCHEN (1405–1477).

Sakya master and prolific author, famous for his work on doxography entitled *Knowing All Tenet Systems* (*grub mtha' kun shes*).

TĀRĀ (Skt.), Tib. *sgrol ma*.

Female bodhisattva, embodiment of the enlightened activity of the buddhas.

THREE HIGHER TRAININGS (*triśikṣā, bslab pa gsum*).

The training in ethical discipline (*śīla, tshul khrims*) by abstaining from unwholesome deeds and practicing positive ones; training in wholesome mental states (*samādhi, ting nge 'dzin*) by stabilizing and refining wholesome mental states like concentration, loving kindness, etc.; and training in wisdom (*prajñā, shes rab*) by learning to see things as they really are.

THREE JEWELS (*triratna, dkon mchog gsum*).
: The three objects of refuge for Buddhists: Buddha, Dharma, and Sangha, also known as the Triple Gem.

THREE KĀYAS. See *kāya*.

THREE VEHICLES. See *vehicles*.

TONGLEN (Tib. *gtong len*).
: Literally, "sending and taking." The practice of mentally exchanging one's own happiness and its causes for others' suffering along with its causes, tonglen is a key practice in the training in relative bodhicitta.

TRIPLE GEM. See *Three Jewels*.

TRI RALPACHEN (r. 815–838).
: The last of the three Dharma Kings of Tibet who strongly supported Buddhism. He supported the standardization of Buddhist terminology and sponsored many translations from Sanskrit to Tibetan.

TRISONG DETSEN (742–797).
: The second of the three Dharma Kings of Tibet, Trisong Detsen was able to firmly establish Buddhism in Tibet with the help Padmasambhava and Śāntarakṣita, and the founding of Samyé Monastery.

TSARPA (Tib. *tshar pa*).
: One of the three main sub-traditions of the Sakya school, founded by Tsarchen Losal Gyatso (1502–1566). It is particularly known for its special lineage of Vajrayoginī practice.

TWELVE LINKS OF DEPENDENT ARISING. See *dependent arising*.

TWO REALITIES (*satyadvaya, bden pa gnyis*).
: According to the Buddha's teachings there are two realities: conventional (*saṁvṛti, kun rdzob*) and ultimate (*paramārtha,*

don dam). Conventional reality is how things appear. It is perceived as real by ordinary beings but seen as illusory by āryas. For the latter, only ultimate reality, that is, the true nature of things, is real. The definition of the two realities varies according to the different schools of thought. For Vaibhāṣikas, for instance, whatever can be broken down into smaller constituent parts—whether physically or by means of mental analysis—is a conventional reality, while that which cannot be broken down any further is ultimately real. In this sense, the *individual person* and *outer phenomena* (such as "mountain," "table," "curry," etc.) are conventional realities, whereas the individual particles constituting physical phenomena and the individual moments of cognition are ultimately real. According to the Madhyamaka view as expounded in the Sakya tradition, conventional reality refers to the phenomena that appear to the mind when the analysis that investigates their ultimate reality is not applied. Ultimate reality is the direct, nonconceptual realization of the true nature of reality free of all conceptual extremes (of existence, nonexistence, both, and neither).

UNIVERSAL GROUND CONSCIOUSNESS (*ālayavijñāna, kun gzhi rnam shes*).

The eighth aspect of consciousness in the eight-consciousness model of the mind according to Yogācāra. Universal ground consciousness is the subtle continuum of mind that continues in an uninterrupted flow, through states of unconsciousness and in-between lives. It is so called because it is the basis for storing the karmic latencies generated by actions of body, speech, and mind, and thus functions as the basis for the experience of their results.

ULTIMATE BODHICITTA. See *bodhicitta*.

ULTIMATE REALITY. See *two realities*.

VAIBHĀṢIKA (Skt.), Tib. *bye brag smra ba*.
Literally, "commentary follower." A subschool of the Hīnayāna based on the *Mahāvibhāṣa*, a collection of seven Abhidharma treatises, the views of which were summarized by Vasubandhu in his *Treasury of Abhidharma*. Based on their peculiar definition of conventional and ultimate reality, the proponents of this school assert a kind of realism, holding that partless particles and indivisible moments of consciousness exist on the ultimate level.

VAIROCANA (Skt.), Tib. *rnam par snang mdzad*.
Vairocana, the "illuminating" Buddha, represents cosmic wisdom and enlightenment and is often depicted at the center of maṇḍalas, seated in meditation posture with his hands placed in the gesture of absorption.

VASUBANDHU (4th–5th century CE).
One of the most influential Buddhist masters of India who authored numerous foundational texts. His *Treasury of Abhidharma* (*Abhidharmakośa*) remains a core text studied in all traditions of Tibet Buddhism.

VEHICLES, THREE (*yāna, theg pa*).
The three paths to liberation taught in accordance with followers' varying capacities: Śrāvakayāna or Vehicle of the Hearers, which was taught to the Buddha's disciples who aspired to gain liberation for themselves; Pratyekabuddhayāna or Vehicle of Solitary Realizers, which is the path to individual liberation taken in times when no buddha taught the Dharma; and Mahāyāna or Great Vehicle, taught to the bodhisattvas who aspire to achieve perfect buddhahood for the sake of others. The Mahāyāna includes the common Pāramitāyāna and the extraordinary Vajrayāna. When the

tantric path of Vajrayāna is listed as a separate vehicle, the three vehicles are Hīnayāna, Mahāyāna, and Vajrayāna.

VIEW (Tib. *lta ba*).

One's fundamental understanding of reality and the nature of phenomena.

VIPAŚYANĀ. See *special insight*.

WHEEL OF BECOMING (*bhavacakra, srid pa'i 'khor lo*).

An iconographic representation of the cycle of existence and rebirth. Traditionally painted on monastery walls, it illustrates the six realms of existence, its three root causes, and the process of dependent arising that keeps the wheel in motion. It is gripped by Yama, the lord of death, symbolizing impermanence.

YAKṢA (Skt.), Tib. *gnod sbyin*.

A class of nature spirits that can be malevolent or benevolent, known for bestowing wealth and worldly boons.

ZHANGTÖN CHÖBAR (1053–1135).

An important master in the Lamdré lineage, Zhangtön Chöbar became one of the principal teachers of Sachen Kunga Nyingpo.

Bibliography

Texts on Parting from the Four Attachments

English Publications

Chogye Trichen Rinpoche. *Parting from the Four Attachments: Jetsun Drakpa Gyaltsen's Song of Experience on Mind Training and the View*. Ithaca, N.Y.: Snow Lion Publications, 2003.

Dzongsar Jamyang Khyentse Rinpoche. *Parting from the Four Attachments: Sachen Kunga Nyingpo's Lojong Shenpa Shidrel, the Mind-training of Parting from the Four Attachments*, with commentary by Dzongsar Jamyang Khyentse Rinpoche. https://khyentsefoundation.org/. Siddhartha's Intent, 2012.

Tibetan Publications

Gorampa Sönam Sengé (*go rams pa bsod nams seng ge*, 1429-1489). *blo sbyong zhen pa bzhi bral gyi khrid yig zab don gnad kyi lde'u mig*. In: Hundred Instructions on Mind Training, vol. 1, 495–508.

Jamyang Khyentse Wangpo (*'jam dbyangs mkhyen brtse'i dbang po*, 1820–1892). *blo sbyong zhen pa bzhi bral gyi nyams dbyangs snying gi bdud rtsi.* In: Treasury of Precious Instructions, vol. 6, 305–307; Collection of Tantras, vol. 23, 535–536.

Jetsün Drakpa Gyaltsen (*rje btsun grags pa rgyal mtshan*, 1147–1216). *zhen pa bzhi bral gyi gdams pa.* In: Treasury of Precious Instructions, vol. 6, 310–314; Collection of Tantras, vol. 23, 482–486; Hundred Instructions on Mind Training, vol. 1, 487–491.

Khenchen Appey Rinpoche. (*mkhan chen a pad yon tan bzang po*, 1927–2010). *theg pa chen po'i sgom khrid kun phan bdud rtsi'i char rgyun.* Kathmandu: International Buddhist Academy, 2015.

Kunga Drolchok (*kun dga 'grol mchog*). *zhen pa bzhi bral gyi khrid yig.* In: Treasury of Precious Instructions, vol. 18, 128–130.

Kunga Lekrin (*kun dga' legs pa'i rin chen*, 15th cent.). *zhen pa bzhi bral gyi khrid yig rje bla ma ā nan+da b+ha dra'i gsung sgros.* In: Treasury of Precious Instructions, vol. 6, 317–342; Collection of Tantras, vol. 23, 492–521; Hundred Instructions on Mind Training, vol. 1, 508–536.

Ngorchen Kunga Zangpo (*ngor chen kun dga' bzang po*, 1382–1456). *zhen pa bzhi bral gyi brgyud 'debs.* In: Treasury of Precious Instructions, vol. 6, 305–307; Collection of Tantras, vol. 23, 489–492.

Ngor Pönlop Ngawang Lekdrup (*ngor dpon slob Ngag dbang legs grub*, 1811–?). *blo sbyong zhen pa bzhi bral gyi khrid byang sems kun dga' legs rin gyis mdzad pa'i 'chad thabs nor bu ke ta ka'i do shal.* In: Treasury of Precious Instructions, vol. 6, 342–356; Collection of Tantras, vol. 23, 521–535.

Nuba Rigdzin Drak (*nub pa rig 'dzin grags*, 12th cent.). *nub pa rig 'dzin grags kyis mdzad pa"i zhen pa bzhi bral*. In: Treasury of Precious Instructions, vol. 6, 315–317; Collection of Tantras, vol. 23, 487–489; Hundred Instructions on Mind Training, vol. 1, 492–495.

Sakya Paṇḍita Kunga Gyaltsen (*sa skya paN+Di ta kun dga'rgyal mtshan*, 1182–1251). *zhen pa bzhi bral gyi gdams pa*. In: Treasury of Precious Instructions, vol. 6, 314–315; Collection of Tantras, vol. 23, 486–487; Hundred Instructions on Mind Training, vol. 1, 491–492.

Tsultrim Palden (*tshul khrims dpal ldan*). *zhen pa bzhi bral gyi 'grel ba rnam grol lam bzang gsal ba'i sgron me*. Dehra Dun: Sa skya rin chen chos gling, 2009 (BDRC MW4CZ74970).

COLLECTIONS

Collection of Tantras, compiled by Ngor Pönlop Loter Wangpo (1847–1914): N. Lungtok & N. Gyaltsan. *rgyud sde kun btus*. Delhi, 2004. (BDRC MW21295; 30 vols.).

Hundred Instructions on Mind Training, compiled by Müchen Könchok Gyaltsen (1388–1469) and Zhönnu Gyalchok (14th cent.): *blo sbyong brgya rtsa sogs*. Kathmandu: sa skya rgyal yongs gsung rab slob gnyer khang, 2007 (BDRC W1KG4285; 2 vols.).

Treasury of Precious Instructions, compiled by Jamgön Kongtrul (1813–1899): *gdams ngag rin po che'i mdzod*. Delhi: Shechen Publications, 1999 (BDRC W23605; 18 vols.).

Sūtra – The Words of the Buddha

Recalling the Three Jewels (*ratnatrayānusmṛti*, dkon mchog gsum rjes su dran pa)
Translation from the Tibetan: Adam Pearcey. *Noble Sūtra of Recalling the Three Jewels.* https://www.lotsawahouse.org/words-of-the-buddha/sutra-recalling-three-jewels. Lotsawa House, 2001.

Taking Refuge in the Three Jewels (*triśaraṇagamana*, gsum la skyabs su 'gro ba).
Translation from the Tibetan: Dharmachakra Translation Committee. *Taking Refuge in the Three Jewels.* Toh 225. https://read.84000.co/translation/toh225.html. 84000: Translating the Words of the Buddha, 2020.

Śāstra - Commentarial Treatises by Indian Masters

Asaṅga. *Compendium of Abhidharma* (*Abhidharmasamuccaya*). See Boin-Webb 2001.

Buddhaghosa. The Path of Purification (*Visuddhimagga*). See Bikkhu Ñāṇamoli 2010.

Candrakirti. *Entering the Middle Way* (*Madhyamakāvatāra*). See Padmakara Translation Group 2002, and Dzongsar Jamyang Khyentse Rinpoche 2003.

Maitreya. *The Ornament of Mahāyāna Sūtras* (*Mahāyānasūtrālaṃkāra*). See Jamspal et al. 2004, Dharmachakra Translation Committee 2014, and Padmakara Translation Group 2018.

Nāgārjuna. *Letter to a Friend* (*Suhṛlekkha*). See Padma Translation Group 2005.

―――. *Precious Garland* (*Ratnāvalī*). See Hopkins 2007.

Śāntideva. *The Way of the Bodhisattva* (*Bodhicaryāvatāra*). See Wallace and Wallace 1997, Padmakara Translation Group 2006, and Lama Kalsang Gyaltsen and Ani Kunga Chodron 2006.

Translations and Secondary Literature

Bikkhu Ñāṇamoli (transl.) *The Path of Purification (Visuddhimagga) by Bhadantācariya Buddhaghosa*. Kandy: Buddhist Publication Society, 2010.

Boin-Webb, Sara (transl.). *Asaṅga. Abhidharmasamuccaya: The Compendium of the Higher Teaching (Philosophy)*. Translated into French by Walpola Rahula. Translated from the French by Sara Boin-Webb. Fremont: Asian Humanities Press, 2001.

Dharmachakra Translation Committee (transl.). *Ornament of the Great Vehicle Sūtras: Maitreya's Mahāyāna-sūtrālaṃkāra with Commentaries by Khenpo Shenga and Ju Mipham*. Boston: Snow Lion, 2014.

Dzongsar Jamyang Khyentse Rinpoche. *Introduction to the Middle Way: Chandrakirtis's Madhyamakavatara with Commentary by Dzongsar Jamyang Khyentse Rinpoche*. Khyentse Foundation, 2003.

Gyurme Dorje (transl.). *Jonang: The One Hundred and Eight Teaching Manuals. Essential Teachings of the Eight Practice Lineages of Tibet, Volume 18 (The Treasury of Precious Instructions)*. Ithaca, N.Y.: Snow Lion Publications, 2021.

Hopkins, Jeffrey (transl.). *Nāgārjuna's Precious Garland: Buddhist Advice for Living and Liberation*. Ithaca, N.Y.: Snow Lion Publications, 2007.

Jackson, David P.: *Clarifying the Sage's Intent: Sakya Paṇḍita's Explanation of the Bodhisattva Path*. In: *Stages of the Buddha's Teachings: Three Key Texts*. Volume 10 in *The Library of Tibetan Classics*. Somerville: Wisdom Publications, 2015.

Jamspal, L. et al. (transl.) *The Universal Vehicle Discourse Literature (Mahāyāna-sūtrālaṁkāra) by Maitreyanātha/ Āryāsaṅga, together with its Commentary (Bhāṣya) by Vasubandhu*. Translated by L. Jamspal, R. Clark, J. Wilson, L. Zwilling, M. Sweet, and R. Thurman. New York: American Institute of Buddhist Studies, 2004.

Khenchen Appey Rinpoche. *Teachings on Sakya Pandita's Clarifying the Sage's Intent*. Kathmandu: Vajra Publications, 2008.

———. *Cultivating a Heart of Wisdom: Oral Instructions on the Mind Training in Seven Points*. In: *Words of a Gentle Sage: Collected Teachings of Khenchen Appey Rinpoche, Volume 1*. Kathmandu: Vajra Books, 2018.

———. *Cultivating the Middle Way: Oral Instructions Based on Candrakīrti's Entering the Middle Way*. In: *Words of a Gentle Sage: Collected Teachings of Khenchen Appey Rinpoche, Volume 2*. Kathmandu: Vajra Books, 2022.

Kunzang Pelden. *The Nectar of Manjushri's Speech: A Detailed Commentary on Śāntideva's Way of the Bodhisattva*. Translated by the Padmakara Translation Group. Boston: Shambhala, 2010.

Lama Kalsang Gyaltsen and Ani Kunga Chodron (transl.). *Bodhisattvacharyavatara: Engaging in the Conduct of the Bodhisattvas with a Commentary by Sazang Mati Panchen*. 2 vols. Walden, N.Y.: Tsechen Kunchab Ling, 2006.

Ngorchen Könchok Lhundrup. *Ornament to Beautify the Three Appearances: The Mahāyāna Preliminary Practices of the Sakya Lamdré Tradition*. Translated by Cyrus Stearns. Boston, MA: Wisdom Publications, 2021.

O'Sullivan, Adrian (transl.). *Bodhicaryāvatāra with Commentary, Śāntideva and Sonam Tsemo*. BookBaby, 2019.

Padmakara Translation Group (transl.). *Introduction to the Middle Way: Chandrakirti's Madhyamakavatara with commentary by Jamgön Mipham*. Boston: Shambhala, 2002.

———. *Nagarjuna's Letter to a Friend with Commentary by Kangyur Rinpoche*. Ithaca, N.Y.: Snow Lion Publications, 2005.

———. *The Way of the Bodhisattva: A Translation of the Bodhicharyāvatāra*. Rev. ed. Boston: Shambhala, 2006.

———. *A Feast of the Nectar of the Supreme Vehicle: An Explanation of the Ornament of the Mahayana Sutras*. Boulder: Shambhala, 2018.

Rhoton, Jared Douglas (transl.). *A Clear Differentiation of the Three Codes: Essential Distinctions among the Individual Liberation, Great Vehicle, and Tantric Systems*. Albany: State University of New York Press, 2002.

Scheuermann, Rolf. *When Sūtra Meets Tantra: Sgam po pa's Four Dharma Doctrine as an Example for his Synthesis of the Bka' gdams- and Mahāmudrā-Systems*. PhD Dissertation. Vienna: Universität Wien, 2015.

Thubten Jinpa (transl.). *Mind Training: The Great Collection*. Boston, MA: Wisdom Publications, 2005.

Wallace, Vesna A. and Wallace, B. Alan (transl.). *A Guide to the Bodhisattva Way of Life (Bodhicaryāvatāra)*. Ithaca, N.Y.: Snow Lion Publications, 1997.